Adventures in Artificial Life

Clayton Walnum

que

Trademarks

All terms mentioned in this book that are known to be trademarks or service marks have been appropriately capitalized. Que cannot attest to the accuracy of this information. Use of a term in this book should not be regarded as affecting the validity of any trademark or service mark.

Publisher: David P. Ewing

Associate Publisher: Rick Ranucci

Operations Manager: Sheila Cunningham

Publishing Plan Manager: Thomas H. Bennett

Marketing Manger: Ray Robinson

Dedication

To Michael Marquis, one of those teachers few students forget.

Credits

Publishing Manager
Joseph B. Wikert

Production Editor
Kezia Endsley

Copy Editor
Phil Kitchel

Technical Editor
Salvatore Mangano

Formatter
Jill L. Stanley

Book Designer
Amy Peppler-Adams

Graphic Image Specialists
Jodie Cantwell
Dennis Sheehan
Susan VandeWalle

Production Team
Danielle Bird
Julie Brown
Paula Carroll
Brook Farling
Heather Kaufman
Bob LaRoche
Jay Lesandrini
Caroline Roop
Linda Seifert
Sandra Shay
Amy Steed
Lillian Yates

Indexer
Johnna Van Hoose

Composed in Stone Serif and MCPdigital
by Prentice Hall Computer Publishing

About the Author

Clayton Walnum has been writing about computers for a decade
and has published over 300 articles in major computer publications.
He is also the author of 12 books, covering such diverse topics as
programming, computer gaming, and application programs. His
most recent book is *QBasic for Rookies,* also published by Que. His
earlier titles include *Borland C++ Power Programming* (Que), *PC
Picasso: A Child's Computer Drawing Kit* (Sams), *The First Book of
Microsoft Works for Windows* (Sams), *PowerMonger: The Official
Strategy Guide* (Prima), and *C-manship Complete* (Taylor Ridge Books).
Mr. Walnum, a full-time free-lance writer, lives in Connecticut with
his wife and their three children.

Acknowledgments

I want to thank the following people for their contributions to
this book: Joe Wikert, Kezia Endsley, Phil Kitchel, and Salvatore
Mangano. And, as always, appreciation goes to my family for their
support.

Overview

Table of Contents

4 Appetite for Destruction: Computer Viruses   65

5 The Silicon Brain: Artificial Intelligence   83

6 Silicon and Steel: The Study of Robotics   101

Wonders on the Edge of Chaos

Welcome to the world of artificial life, where reality and science fiction collide head on and meld to create a place where human-kind's wildest dreams or worst nightmares can come to pass. Whether artificial life (or a-life, as it's affectionately called) provides us with a wonderful new future or the extinction of life as we know it is all in the hands of a few scientists. These scientists are, even as you read this paragraph, delving deeper and deeper into this new area of scientific research.

In this book, you meet many of the scientists whose discoveries have moved us closer to the day when computer-generated organisms might actually be considered alive. You learn about everything from simple simulations of one-celled organisms to super-intelligent robots that might one day decide they no longer need the human race in their world. Along the way, you see how artificial-life programs work and even experiment first-hand with some examples of artificial life included on this book's disk.

If nothing else, this book makes you think; it forces you to consider some viewpoints with which you've never been confronted before. Although many of the issues presented in the following pages are philosophical in nature today, a time will arrive when they must be faced and resolved. What is life? Can a computer program ever actually be alive? Is it possible to create human-like intelligence on a computer? Need we fear studies of artificial life? The answers to these questions will surprise, thrill, shock, and in many cases, disturb you.

An Overview of this Book

This book covers not only "traditional" forms of artificial life, but also several related topics. The following briefly outlines each chapter of *Adventures in Artificial Life*:

- *Chapter 1, "The God Game: An Introduction to Artificial Life,"* offers an introduction to the field of artificial life. Included here is a comparison of biological and artificial life, as well as a brief discussion of a few relevant philosophical issues.

- *Chapter 2, "Seeds of Creation: The History of Artificial Life,"* explores the history of artificial-life studies, with a concentration on Christopher Langton's work and Thomas Ray's Tierra. Other artificial life studies also are briefly covered.

- *Chapter 3, "A View from Within: How A-Life Works,"* describes some techniques used to create and control artificial life. Covered here are rule-based systems, finite-state automata, neural networks, and genetic algorithms.

- *Chapter 4, "Appetite for Destruction: Computer Viruses,"* introduces you to the dark side of artificial life, discussing various types of computer viruses and their effect on the future of computing. Discussions include the way computer viruses work, how they are spread, and how to avoid them.

- *Chapter 5, "The Silicon Brain: Artificial Intelligence,"* provides an overview of the field of artificial intelligence. This chapter covers the debate between symbolic and non-symbolic approaches to artificial intelligence. In addition, you learn about expert systems, and more about neural networks and computer learning.

- *Chapter 6, "Silicon and Steel: The Study of Robotics,"* explores the science of robotics, including discussions of robot intelligence, knowledge representations, robotic vision, and tactile sensing. Some extraordinary future scenarios also are presented.

- *Chapter 7, "Worlds of Imagination: Virtual Reality,"* provides an overview of virtual reality. Topics include virtual-reality hardware and the uses of virtual reality in the real world. Also discussed is the use of 3-D, real-time modeling to create virtual-reality environments on a computer display.

- *Chapter 8, "A-Life Off the Shelf—Commercial A-Life Programs,"* discusses several artificial life-related programs that you can purchase at your software dealer. Programs reviewed include SimAnt and SimLife, as well as desktop virtual-reality programs like Ultima Underworld and Virtual Reality Studio 2.0. Expert systems, like Home Medical Adviser, also are discussed.

- *Chapter 9, "A Brave and Uncertain New World: The Future of Artificial Life,"* summarizes the main points in the book and discusses the advantages and dangers of artificial life. Possible future scenarios, both positive and negative, are presented. The aim is to give you an appreciation for the complex ethical issues involved in any study of life, whether it be natural or synthetic.

- *Appendix A, Bibliography,* acknowledges the sources used in the writing of this book, as well as provides a list of books and articles for further reading.

Free Software!

Talking about artificial life is one thing, but rolling up your sleeves and conducting your own a-life experiments will help bring home the many topics presented in this book. For this reason, the accompanying disk contains several varieties of a-life programs, as well as games that learn, expert systems, and even a sample of desktop virtual reality.

To install the disk, see the last page of the book (facing the disk). The disk includes the following software:

- *Conway's Game of Life*—With this program, which has both DOS and Windows versions, you create colonies of one-celled animals and watch as they live and die according to the rules of their universe.

- *MicroAnt*—This program enables you to conduct genetic experiments on a colony of ants. You watch ants evolve from clumsy creatures that can barely survive to insects that know exactly how to find what they need to live.

● *Nervous System Construction Kit*—This program shows how scientists use neural networks to simulate the behavior of a cockroach. Use the program's simple editor to create new environments for your roach, or activate the recording feature to create mini-movies of your roach in action.

● *Virus Simulation Suite*—This group of programs gives you a chance to see some infamous computer viruses in action— without risking the infection of your computer system.

● *Guess the Animal*—This intelligent program learns to identify virtually any animal you can think of. The program starts with only limited knowledge of the animal kingdom, but it quickly learns any new animals with which it's presented.

● *Fishing Expert System*—This sample expert system can advise you on your next fishing trip. Just answer a few questions, and the Fishing Expert System tells you the best fishing techniques to use.

● *Virtual Reality Demo*—Fly around in a three-dimensional world with this amazing example of desktop virtual reality. View the virtual-reality world from any angle, using an on-screen control panel to pilot your alien spacecraft from one place to another.

The Adventure Begins

Now that you know what to expect, it's time to climb aboard the tour bus, strap in tightly, and prepare to venture into the great unknown. Always remember that the creatures you're about to see— organisms created within the silicon chips of a computer—are like nothing you've experienced before and are infamously unpredictable.

And whether you believe that these computer-generated organisms are actually alive or that such an idea is an argument for philosophers, one thing is for sure: The quest you're about to begin is an adventure you'll never forget.

The God Game: An Introduction to Artificial Life

One of the most popular themes in science fiction literature is the introduction of artificial life forms into human society. From supercomputers that develop god complexes to armies of indestructible robots that enslave humankind, the question of what would happen if we had to share our world with artificial life has fascinated writers for decades. Often, these stories portray a grim future, with the human race fighting for its very existence against creatures of its own creation.

You can find examples of such cautionary tales in just about any collection of science fiction stories. Popular films have also adopted this intriguing theme. Perhaps the most famous artificial life form to run amok is the supercomputer HAL 9000 (from the Academy Award-winning film *2001: A Space Odyssey*), which, due to contradictions in its programming, kills all but one crew member of the spaceship *Discovery*. Who can forget HAL's cool "I'm sorry, Dave. I'm afraid I can't do that," when ordered by Commander David Bowman to open the pod bay doors and allow the commander back into the Discovery? (*2001: A Space Odyssey* was written by Arthur C. Clarke, inspired by his short story "The Sentinel," and is also available as a novel.)

As exciting as these harrowing tales might be, science fiction stories also frequently portray the human race living peacefully alongside artificial life forms. For example, the late Isaac Asimov built a large readership around his robot stories. Asimov governed his sophisticated robots by the Three Laws of Robotics:

1. A robot may not injure a human being, or through inaction, allow a human being to come to harm.

2. A robot must obey the orders given it by human beings except when such orders conflict with the First Law.

3. A robot must protect its existence as long as such protection does not conflict with the First or Second Law.

Yet, Asimov was a master at creating mysteries in which, due to unforeseen conflicts with the three laws, his robots acted in seemingly inexplicable ways.

For those who like their fiction to take an idea to the limits of the imagination, James P. Hogan's fascinating book *Code of the Life Maker* depicts a world in which living machines have naturally evolved from the remains of a crashed factory ship. Finally, in the grim novel, *Blood Music,* author Greg Bear tells of a scientist who creates a microscopic computer "biochip," which, after being injected into the human bloodstream, mutates into an intelligent microorganism that eventually destroys the human race.

Do these tales seem far-fetched? Perhaps they are. But every day, scientists get closer to creating artificial life forms that previously existed only in the pages of these science fiction tales. If that fact makes you uneasy, you'll understand why these same scientists are so concerned with the results of their studies, as well as with developing a code of ethics to govern the field in which they've chosen to work.

What is life? Are artificial life forms actually alive? And, if so, do artificial life forms have the same right to life as humans? How can we ensure that we retain control over artificial life once it's created?

These and many other questions are much debated, and the answers aren't as obvious as one might think. It's easy to discount all artificially created life forms—especially those of the computer-based variety—as merely lifeless constructions. But any definition of life is vague at best. Who ultimately has the dubious honor of deciding what is alive and what is not?

In this chapter, you'll look briefly at the different forms of artificial life currently in existence. Although it's doubtful that any of these creations can actually be considered alive, you'll use them as examples to show how the fine line between what is and what isn't life is difficult, if not impossible, to define. To that end, you'll also examine a definition of life in order to contrast and compare biological and artificial life. Finally, you'll learn about possible applications for artificial life and examine the dangers inherent in the creation of such life forms.

Artificial Life in the Real World

Although scientists develop artificial life forms biologically in genetics labs, the term artificial life (*a-life*) as I use it in this book usually refers to "creatures" that exist within a computer's memory. (This grouping includes the so-called "intelligent robots," which are actually controlled by computers.) Computer a-life can be as simple as a colony of single-celled creatures learning basic behaviors according to simple rules or as complex as an entire virtual world populated with myriad artificial organisms, all competing for resources as in the real world.

A popular computer pastime, Conway's Game of Life, is an example of the simplest computer a-life. In this simulation, one-celled creatures vie for living space according to a small set of mathematical rules. Much like bacteria growing in a petri dish, cells rapidly live and die in a blur of colored patterns. (See Figure 1.1.)

Maxis Software's impressive SimLife, on the other hand, is a commercially available a-life program in which users create an entire biosphere populated with sophisticated plant and animal life forms of their own design. In SimLife, the user can modify each life form's genetic characteristics or fiddle with the environment to see what effect it has on the created creatures. This program is similar (although presented in game form) to the programs used by some researchers studying a-life.

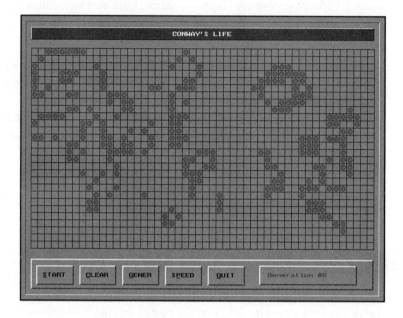

Conway's Game of Life. One-celled organisms live and die according to a simple set of rules.

One form of a-life with which you might have had experience is the *computer virus*. Although biologists have yet to decide whether biological viruses are actually living organisms, viruses do boast some of the characteristics of life, most importantly the capability to reproduce. Like their biological counterparts, computer viruses are highly skilled in reproduction. A single copy of a computer virus released on the unsuspecting public can soon infect thousands, possibly even millions, of machines. Moreover, to simulate the incubation time required for most disease viruses, many computer viruses are capable of lying in wait, unknown to the infected systems, until certain criteria are met, after which they activate their destructive capabilities.

Two other topics related to a-life in this book are *robotics* and *virtual reality*. Although robots sophisticated enough to qualify as artificial life might seem like something from the distant future, recent advances in artificial intelligence coupled with the ever-growing field of electronics and mechanics bring that future closer every day.

Unlike robotics, which deals mostly with physical constructions that mimic certain human abilities, virtual reality eschews the physical and instead creates electronic fantasy worlds you can visit—with the help of sophisticated computers and electronic gear (Figure 1.2).

Figure 1.2.

Virtual reality plunges the user into a computer-controlled fantasy world.

NOTE: When the term *artificial life* is used in this book, it does not necessarily refer to living creatures, but rather to creations that simulate life. Still, words tend to gain new meaning over time. The word *intelligent,* for example, was once used to describe machines only in speculative fiction. Today, computer scientists use the word *intelligent* regularly to describe computers and computer programs. Will we soon see a similar new meaning for the word *living*?

The Role of Artificial Intelligence

As you've probably guessed, artificial intelligence (*AI*) plays a huge role in the study of computer a-life, but not always in ways you might expect. For example, AI is more often used to control a simulation than to create creatures that actually seem intelligent. It takes a wealth of computing power to apply the rules of a sophisticated simulation, track the values of the variables involved, and interpret the results in a meaningful way. AI algorithms incorporate computational objects such as finite state automatons and neural networks (both of which you'll learn about later in this book) to solve the many problems with which they're presented.

When you think of artificial intelligence, however, you might imagine something more flamboyant than a control device for simulations. You might imagine fantastic computers (like the aforementioned HAL 9000) with fully developed psyches and personalities; machines that not only think and respond like humans, but also display emotions and self-awareness. You might even imagine intelligent robots obeying your every command: scuttling about your home, cooking, cleaning, taking care of the kids, and satisfying every human whim. The control of such robots is another possible application for artificial intelligence.

AI routines also control virtual reality (VR) systems, which plunge you into a computer-controlled simulated environment so real that, for all intents and purposes, you're there. These systems provide a total sensory illusion that includes not only three-dimensional visuals, but also realistic sound and even the capability to touch, feel, and interact with the imaginary objects around you. Although VR does not constitute artificial life, a fully realized VR system should incorporate computer-controlled beings that simulate people.

In short, artificial intelligence and a-life are often closely related. In fact, sophisticated a-life cannot exist without clever AI algorithms to handle the complexities of the simulation.

Researchers Speak Out About A-Life

Judging by its fantastic nature, you might have the urge to tuck a-life away with controversial subjects like ESP and UFOs. That would be a mistake. The study of artificial life is well respected, with many leading researchers lending their efforts to the advancement of the field. Perhaps the most well-known researcher is computer scientist and a-life pioneer Christopher Langton, who works at the Los Alamos National Laboratory in New Mexico. Does Langton take a-life seriously? You bet. According to Langton, a-life is destined to become an important part of a new biosphere that includes traditional and artificial life forms (Figure 1.3). He says further that humans will have to develop a new culture in which biological life and a-life learn to cooperate for the benefit of both.

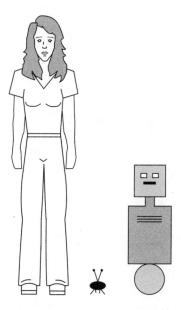

Figure 1.3.

Artificial life is destined to become an important part of a new biosphere.

Doyne Farmer, a physicist at the Santa Fe Institute in New Mexico, says that within the next century living organisms created by humans will almost certainly be a part of our world. These human-made organisms will have the capability to reproduce and evolve, just like other organisms.

Thomas S. Ray, an evolutionary biologist and the creator of a computer world called Tierra, insists that, because his a-life creatures have evolved on their own, they represent an actual synthesis of life rather than simply a simulation. The results he has obtained with Tierra have forced many scientists to at least question their definitions of life.

On the robotics front, Rodney Brooks, who conducts his studies in the mobile robot lab at MIT, refers to his robotic creations as "real artificial life." One of his robots gathers and disposes of soft-drink cans. Another sells candy and then uses the proceeds to buy services from humans. If you happen to step into Brooks' lab, you might be startled by a tiny shape scurrying for cover. This is Squirt, one of Brooks' robotic insects, which exhibits such bug-like behaviors as avoiding light and sound and searching for hiding places.

What all these researchers have in common is a belief that real artificial life is not only possible, but inevitable—that the human race will soon have to make room in their world for strange new residents. One thing is for sure: Whether these new creations are actually alive will be the subject of much heated debate.

What Exactly Is Life?

Scientists have long searched for the perfect definition of life. So far, this definition has eluded them. Although you can examine an object and decide whether or not it's alive, stating why you've come to that decision is no simple task. As you list potential characteristics of life, you quickly run into exceptions and complications. Very specific definitions of life, for example, often leave out some real forms of life, whereas general definitions tend to include objects that are not truly living. The truth is, scientists might never fully agree on what constitutes life. When one considers the wide variety of living things on this planet, it's not surprising that a comprehensive definition is not easily forthcoming.

One might be tempted to say, for example, that all living things must reproduce. But what about mules? Mules are sterile, incapable of reproduction. Are they then not living? As you can see, while this

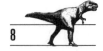

definition of life leaves out computers and other machines, it also leaves out some living creatures.

One might also be tempted to say that a life form must gather information and act on the information in some way. Although this is true of all living things, it's also true of a thermostat. Is a thermostat alive?

Despite the difficulty of defining life, guidelines have to be established, even if they're not perfect. So, for the sake of the following discussion, assume that all life must have the following four characteristics:

1. *Structure.* Every living thing must have a characteristic form that differentiates it from other living things. For example, cats must look like cats and dogs must look like dogs.

2. *Reproduction.* All living things must reproduce. True, a mule cannot reproduce directly. However, mules can be produced by mating a horse with a donkey. A living thing without some reproductive mechanism is quickly doomed to extinction.

3. *Energy processing.* All living things must consume some form of energy and excrete a waste product. Plants, for example, absorb sunlight and excrete oxygen.

4. *Information processing.* All life forms must gather information about their environment and react accordingly. When a dog feels hot, it moves out of the sun. When a person walking down the street comes to an obstruction, she walks around it.

Maybe these four characteristics of life (Figure 1.4) aren't perfect, but they're close enough to use in a comparison of biological and artificial life. Because there's little question that all biological life shares the aforementioned characteristics, you can examine how these characteristics fit a sophisticated computer. Computers are, after all, the common element in all forms of a-life discussed in this book.

Computer systems definitely have structure. Moreover, it's a structure that easily distinguishes one type of computer from another. A Macintosh looks different from an IBM-compatible, for example, and an Amiga looks different from an Atari.

Figure 1.4.

All living things share four characteristics: structure, reproduction, energy processing, and information processing.

As for reproduction, although machines don't reproduce in the way animals or plants do, there are abundant examples of machines that build machines. Robots perform a variety of assembly tasks, and these robotic assembly systems are increasingly less dependent on human assistance. (The NEXT computer factory, for example, used a great deal of automation in the production of the NEXT computer.) Some can run 24 hours a day with only minimal supervision. If robots can build other machines, haven't they satisfied the reproduction requirement in the same indirect way as animals like mules?

Computers are certainly energy processing machines. They don't eat food, but they consume electricity and excrete heat as a waste product.

Of course, computers process information. Moreover, with the appropriate peripherals, computers can easily sense elements of their environment and act on them. In fact, humans probably use computers for this activity more than for any other. Computers monitor automobiles, home heating systems, security systems, and any number of other complex environment control systems.

So, computer systems have structure, as well as process both energy and information (Figure 1.5). When we develop machinery that can build computers with no human intervention, thus providing a reproductive mechanism, computers will meet the basic criteria for life.

Figure 1.5.

Computer systems have structure, as well as process both energy and information.

So, are computers alive? Not so far. However, you can quickly see that, when you apply the characteristics of life with an open mind, the line between the living and the nonliving is a fuzzy one indeed.

Can You Recognize Life When You See It?

Having an open mind is important when examining the characteristics of life. When trying to determine whether a new creation is indeed alive, you must take care that your judgment is not affected by biases and preconceptions. Currently, you might believe you have a solid understanding of what constitutes life, but future life with which humans might come in contact might take on entirely different forms, might in fact be based on an entirely different chemistry.

Although life as you know it is carbon-based, who's to say that it is the only viable form? Would you recognize life that evolved on another world, under different environmental conditions than those on Earth? It's possible that such a life form would be so alien to us that we wouldn't consider it living any more than we consider a rock living. But we'd be wrong. Not considering something to be alive because it doesn't fit within our sphere of experience is egocentric—bigotry in its purest form.

Most people don't consider computers living, of course; not as we know them today. However, a good scientist knows that this preconceived notion must be treated with suspicion. It must be tested every step of the way as we move toward a future that might include many forms of artificial life. Where do we draw the line between a conventional computer and one so sophisticated that it might be considered a living being?

In 1950, Alan M. Turing published a paper called "Computing Machinery and Intelligence." In his paper, Turing presented a test to judge the effectiveness of various artificial intelligence algorithms. The Turing Test implies that if a person can't tell the difference between a machine and a human, the machine is a human-like organism.

In the Turing Test, a person talks via a keyboard with both a computer and a human, not knowing which is which. By asking questions and evaluating the answers, the person must determine which subject is the computer and which is the human. You may think this would be easy, but programmers have become so adept at simulating intelligence that it's often difficult to differentiate the answers.

Of course, something need not be intelligent to be alive. However, intelligence is certainly a characteristic that one associates with higher forms of life, including not only humans but also apes, dolphins, and whales. A clever program capable of providing human-like answers to questions is not living (at least, not necessarily). The Turing Test, however, demonstrates that one characteristic associated with being alive can be effectively simulated on a machine—an object normally classified as not living.

Human or Machine?

Case in point: In 1991 at the Computer Museum in Boston, the first annual Loebner Prize Competition took place. In this competition, computer programs were tested to determine which most excelled at the Turing Test (Figure 1.6). During the test, expert judges moved from terminal to terminal, typing questions and evaluating answers. The program that won the competition (PC Therapist, written by Joseph Weintraub of Thinking Software) fooled five out of the 10 judges, an impressive achievement when you consider that you have the same odds by simply flipping a coin.

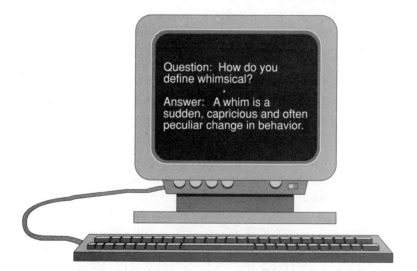

Question: How do you define whimsical?

Answer: A whim is a sudden, capricious and often peculiar change in behavior.

Figure 1.6.

The Turing Test. Is the subject human or machine? In this case, based on a response from PC Therapist, it's a machine.

Why Study Artificial Life?

Scientists don't study a-life simply to satisfy a few researchers' curiosities. A-life offers a number of practical applications that can

13

help life on Mother Earth be much easier. At the very least, the study of a-life helps scientists develop tools for learning more about biological life. By using complex simulations comprising artificial environments and the computerized organisms that dwell there, scientists can study how life forms evolve and learn.

It's impossible to turn back the clock on the real world, but by recording the starting point of a simulation, scientists can run the same simulation many times. They can introduce changes to either the environment or to the genetic makeup of the organisms, and analyze the results. They can repeat tests under exactly the same conditions as many times as needed to verify results—an important element of scientific research. In these artificial worlds, the scientist can fully control weather, food availability, predators, chemical influences, and any number of variables that are difficult, if not impossible, to handle accurately in the real world.

Entertainment is another application for a-life. Every day, computer games become more and more sophisticated. As their sophistication increases, so does the reality of the worlds they simulate. Computer opponents become more intelligent; not only more adept at applying the rules of a game and formulating successful strategies, but also in providing the human player with a *virtual* companion, a gaming partner not unlike the person next door. Transfer these super-intelligent computer routines into a virtual reality setting, and you have fully realized artificial worlds in which anything is possible, in which your most outrageous and wonderful dreams can come to life, fully populated with creatures almost indistinguishable from the real thing (Figure 1.7).

The study of a-life also can yield creatures to help supervise our world and perhaps clean up some of our messes. For example, maybe one day we'll see tiny robotic creatures that "eat" certain types of chemicals or materials. Just as the bacteria in a yogurt culture can change milk into yogurt, so can these new creatures reduce oil spills to a form not threatening to the environment. Such a form of a-life could, like bacteria, be self-replicating. We'd need only release a few into a troubled area, after which they'd reproduce to create a population large enough to handle the problem.

Figure 1.7.

Virtual reality combined with super-sophisticated artificial intelligence will enable humans to play games against strange opponents.

If the idea of releasing a self-replicating artificial life form into the world makes you nervous, you're not alone. Even today, with the study of a-life in its infancy, scientists are developing not only new techniques for creating a-life, but also a set of ethics by which to govern their future discoveries. Just as we conduct genetic studies on microorganisms in carefully controlled environments, lest some potentially dangerous organism escape, so must we carefully control computerized a-life. Computer viruses are a perfect example of the damage that ensues when one enables a-life to run rampant. It might be as difficult to eradicate these tiny self-replicating computer programs as it is to eradicate any other type of disease.

In a worst-case scenario, the creation of a-life might lead to an artificial organism that actually threatens the survival of the human race. Consider the microscopic biochips in the aforementioned novel *Blood Music,* for example. The study of a-life isn't the first time that new technology has presented a threat, of course. Since the 1940s we've lived with, and hopefully managed to control, nuclear devices of various kinds. Researchers in a-life know that the results of their studies can lead to unpredictable outcomes in the near future, so they are working to ensure that their creations can't get out of control.

Conclusion

Whether you believe that artificial life represents a fantastic new future or simply a dead end, there's no denying that it's fascinating stuff. You did buy this book, after all! In the following chapters, you'll examine various types of artificial life as they exist today and as they might exist tomorrow. You even have a chance to do some hands-on research of your own as you explore the programs included on this book's disk. But everything starts at the beginning. In the next chapter, you begin your adventures in artificial life by learning more about some of the influential people in the field.

Seeds of Creation: The History of Artificial Life

Throughout recorded history and probably even long before, human beings have been intrigued with the idea of bestowing life on inanimate objects. In Chapter 1, you read about some examples of artificial life in modern science fiction, but ancient myths also abound with tales of human-made creatures. In Jewish legend, for example, Rabbi Loew of Prague created a being from clay and brought it to life by placing under its tongue a piece of paper on which he had written the name of God.

As for computer-based a-life, its history reaches back only 40 years or so, when John von Neumann, a mathematician and early computer scientist, designed a computer "organism" that could reproduce much like a real creature.

John Conway

 pproximately 30 years ago, an English fellow named John Conway created one of the first a-life simulations to actually run on a computer. Although the rules he invented for a system that simulated the lives of special one-celled animals were simple ones, the results were fascinating. In fact, before long, every computer scientist worthy of his or her diploma had written a version of Conway's Game of Life and spent hours trying different combinations of cells to see what patterns might emerge.

Today, people are still fascinated by Conway's computer simulation. (At the end of this chapter, you see Conway's Game of Life in action.) Many computer science books mention the Game of Life, and each year thousands of computer science students write versions of the Game of Life as part of their programming curriculum. The simplest implementations result in programs that accurately portray the simulation, but run too slowly to be practical. Other implementations blaze across the screen in vivid colors and kaleidoscopic patterns, hypnotizing any viewer that happens to glance in its direction.

When Conway created his simple simulation, he couldn't have imagined how far computer scientists would take his basic idea. Many people have since contributed to the study of a-life, creating sophisticated simulations that make Conway's humble, though fascinating, program look like a child's toy (Figure 2.1). In this chapter, you meet some of the most important people in the field and learn about some of their amazing studies.

However, von Neumann never actually implemented his complex program, and although other computer scientists refined the design, it remained on paper until Christopher Langton, the leading figure in a-life studies today, discovered it in the late 1970s.

Christopher Langton

A-life as an accepted field of study didn't experience its genesis until 1987, when Christopher Langton (Figure 2.2) organized the first workshop on artificial life in New Mexico. The story of how Chris Langton grew from a hippie who wanted to have his own rock band to the leader of a-life studies is as fascinating as a-life itself.

It all started when Langton, having conscientious-objector status during the Vietnam war, served his alternative service (a required service that replaces military service obligations) at Massachusetts General Hospital. His job involved shuffling cadavers between the morgue and the autopsy room. Langton's entire future changed one dreary night when a corpse sat up on its stretcher and shrieked, sending one orderly racing from the room and leaving Langton alone and quivering in his boots. Although Langton is the first to admit that the episode was undoubtedly a sick practical joke (Langton had just finished watching the cult-classic horror film *The Night of the Living Dead,* so the timing was perfect), he refused to return to the morgue and was reassigned to the hospital's computer department.

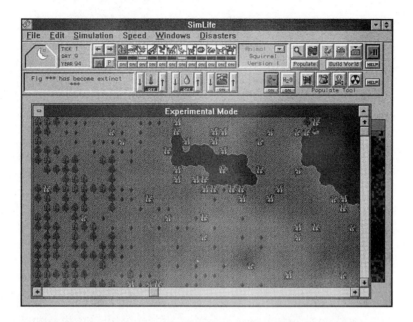

Figure 2.1.

Conway's Game of Life looks like a child's toy when compared with today's simulations, such as Maxis' incredible SimLife.

Photo courtesy of Los Alamos National Laboratory

Figure 2.2.

Christopher Langton is credited for establishing the study of artificial life as an accepted scientific field.

In his new job, he had to design a program that allowed the hospital's computer to run programs written for other types of computers. (This type of program is called an *emulator.*) It was while he worked on this difficult task that he realized the power of a computer, especially for simulating real-world processes. It was also then that he saw his first version of Conway's famous Game of Life—he began thinking about life in terms of a computer simulation.

Although he remained fascinated with the idea of computer-simulated life forms, it wasn't until 1975 that another extraordinary event placed him firmly on the path toward that 1987 a-life conference in New Mexico—and almost killed him in the bargain. Langton, who was returning to school in the fall to pursue his interests, spent the summer with some friends hang gliding in the Blue Ridge Mountains. On his last day before returning to school, the wind died and the airborne Langton plummeted to the ground, breaking 35 bones, puncturing a lung, and crushing his face.

As Langton lay in a hospital bed hovering between consciousness and unconsciousness, his mind suddenly filled with complex information patterns, data entities that seemed almost alive. He spent five months in the hospital, recuperating and thinking about the strange vision and how it related to his fascination with computer life. Langton began reading voraciously on every subject related to simulating biology on a computer. By the time he made it to the University of Arizona almost a year after his accident, he knew exactly what he wanted to do with his life.

Unfortunately, the university offered no formal course of study related to artificial life. The concept of artificial life was not yet an accepted field of research; it existed mostly in Langton's mind. The field encompassed a number of subjects, including computer science, biology, evolution, genetics, mathematics, and even philosophy. As a result, Langton often signed up for as many as 20 courses a semester, and after attending the first few classes of each, dropped those that didn't apply to his studies.

Not surprisingly, Langton's unusual ideas were taken lightly by academia. In fact, after completing his undergraduate work, the University of Michigan was the only school in the country that offered him graduate studies. In spite of his slow start, however,

Langton's ideas eventually attracted interest, and he began publishing papers in scientific journals. These papers drew the attention of Doyne Farmer of the Theoretical Division of the Los Alamos National Laboratory in New Mexico. Farmer was so enthralled by Langton's ideas that he immediately recommended Langton for a fellowship at the laboratory. Langton had, at last, found his home.

In 1987, shortly after starting at the institute, Langton organized the first artificial life workshop, bringing together over 150 scientists who shared Langton's fascination. At the conference, attendees discussed their findings and began forming guidelines for their study. Along with their ideas, scientists also brought their computer creations, including fish, birds, plants, rabbits, foxes, and bees, all of which portrayed certain lifelike behaviors and characteristics.

Although many researchers have developed important theories, Langton's "life on the edge of chaos" theory, presented in his doctoral thesis, has garnered much praise. Langton's theory postulates that there is a narrow range of specific circumstances in which complex systems can develop. To back up his assertions, Langton used computer simulations like Conway's Game of Life, measuring the points in the simulation when the most complex patterns emerged. He theorizes that when little movement can occur, such as in the molecules of ice, the data exchange that allows complex systems like life cannot be supported. On the other hand, too much movement, such as that found in the molecules of steam, also prevents this critical information exchange. It's the narrow area between these extremes, exemplified by the liquid state, in which complex systems such as life can emerge.

Langton firmly believes that life should not be defined by its chemical components but by its organization and activity. For example, how is a cockroach, a simple organism programmed by instinct to respond to its environment in certain ways, different than a computer programmed to do the same thing (Figure 2.3)? Neither a roach nor a computer has a sense of "self"—both are merely machines designed to perform programmed tasks. Is it enough to say that, because a roach is a carbon-based organism, it is living, whereas the computer, which is not carbon-based, is not living?

Figure 2.3.

How is a cockroach—a simple organism programmed by instinct to respond to its environment in certain ways—different than a computer programmed to do the same thing?

Thomas Ray

Thomas Ray, an evolutionary biologist, began his scientific career in a self-built laboratory in Costa Rica, where he researched evolution and ecology in the rain forests. Now, as a professor at the University of Delaware and a researcher at the Santa Fe Institute, he's studying evolution not in the rain forest but on computers. Ray's claim to fame is a computerized world called Tierra, populated with self-replicating computer programs that vie for computer time (representing energy) and computer memory (representing resources).

Although Ray started Tierra with only a single artificial organism, other unexpected organisms quickly evolved, triggered by the mutation functions that Ray built into Tierra. One type of mutation, designed to simulate the effects of environmental factors such as solar radiation, occurs when a bit in a creature's program is randomly flipped. Other types of mutations occur during reproduction, including replication errors that can slightly change the resultant program or even completely scramble an organism's instructions.

Various types of parasites evolved (Figure 2.4), relying on other organisms' programs to reproduce. The first parasites to appear grab the copy programs from hosts, reproducing much the way natural viruses do. As in the natural world, however, hosts in Tierra soon develop immunity to the parasites. This immunity in turn causes the parasites to develop new ways of snatching the code they need—a cycle all too familiar in the real world.

Photo courtesy of the Santa Fe Institute

Figure 2.4.

In this visualization of Tierra, a parasite reproduces by copying a host's copying instructions.

One creature called a *hyperparasite* turns the tables on normal parasites, tricking them into producing hyperparasites instead. This behavior soon drives the normal parasites into extinction, after which the hyperparasites happily cooperate to reproduce each other, forming communities that display simple social behaviors. *Hyper-hyperparasites* eager to take on the status quo then develop, stealing energy that passes between the hyperparasites. Other anomalies that appear in Tierra include *liars,* which misrepresent the size of their programs to gain extra computer time.

No matter how well the organisms in Tierra learn to cope with their environment, life doesn't last forever. Organisms in Tierra age, and when their time is up, a program called the Reaper (see Figure 2.5) takes them off to that big computer in the sky. The Reaper also cleans up defective creatures—organisms unable to function due to scrambled programs—that tend to clutter Tierra's digital landscape. Even in Tierra, Darwin rules the roost.

According to Ray (Figure 2.6), the important aspect of Tierra is that none of the organisms that evolved—parasites, hyperparasites, and so on—were a part of Tierra's original design. They evolved on their own, with no further input from humans. Because of this self-generated evolution, he says that Tierra represents a synthesis of life, rather than a simulation.

Figure 2.5.

In another visualization of Tierra, the Reaper destroys old or defective creatures. The lightning represents mutation, which causes new species of creatures to appear.

Photo courtesy of the Santa Fe Institute

Figure 2.6.

Thomas Ray believes that his Tierra represents a synthesis of life, rather than a simulation.

Photo by Cary Herz

Other Experiments Conducted in A-Life

Although Christopher Langton and Thomas Ray have garnered a lot of attention, many other fine researchers have lent their talents to the research of a-life. For example, Danny Hillis of Thinking Machines Corporation in Cambridge, Massachusetts wrote a program that uses Darwin-like processes to improve the problem-solving capabilities of software, a study that could lead to self-improving programs. Again, it's survival of the fittest—the programs (in this case, sorting programs) doing the best job survive to the next generation. Hillis' computer world also includes organisms represented by ever more difficult sorting problems that constantly challenge the evolving sorting programs.

Robert Collins at the University of California, Los Angeles has created a simulation called ArtAnt in which evolving ant-like organisms compete for survival by learning to find food and avoid conflict. Collins' Ants have 10,000-bit (a bit is the smallest piece of information a computer can process) computer-based chromosomes that control each ant's response to its environment. Mutating chromosomes lead to new types of ants with new capabilities that may or may not increase their chances of survival.

In Chapter 1, you read about Rodney Brooks, who conducts his studies in the mobile robot lab at MIT. His talented robots include one that gathers and disposes of soft drink cans, one that sells candy and uses its earnings to pay humans for services, and robot insects that avoid light and sound.

Craig Reynolds of Symbolics Inc., has created *bird-oid* objects or *boids,* creatures governed by three simple rules: Keep a specific distance from other boids, fly the same speed as other boids, and fly toward the greatest number of boids. Although Reynolds' simulation has no fixed starting point—that is, each boid's position and direction is randomly generated—boids quickly form flocks and demonstrate lifelike behaviors (Figure 2.7). For example, in one run of the simulation, a boid that somehow got separated from the flock "woke up" and zipped back to join the rest. Another crashed into an obstacle, faltered as if stunned, then shot back to join the flock.

Nothing in the program called for these behaviors, which demonstrates how even simple rules, when applied to a large population, can yield unexpected results. (These unexpected results are called *emergent behavior*.)

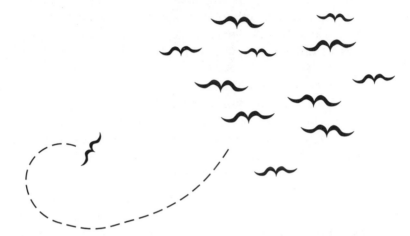

Figure 2.7.

Reynolds' boids demonstrate lifelike behaviors as they flock according to a simple set of rules.

David Jefferson at UCLA is renowned for his program in which rabbits and foxes compete for survival. Each animal has genes that control its size, speed, litter number, and other factors. Like Reynolds' boids, each rabbit and fox in Jefferson's experiment follows a simple set of rules. The rules for a rabbit are 1) If a fox is in its current square, the rabbit must go to a safer square; 2) If grass is in its square, the rabbit must eat; and 3) When a rabbit reaches a specific weight, it reproduces. The similar rules for foxes are 1) Find nearby rabbits; 2) Eat rabbits; and 3) Reproduce after attaining a specific weight.

Mutation (a random change in an organism's genotype), coupled with genetic inheritance, determines the abilities of all rabbit offspring, with the foxes acting as an environmental factor that forces evolution. The simple system works. At the start of the simulation, most rabbits are slow and unable to avoid foxes. Sooner or later, however, thanks to mutation, a faster rabbit appears. Because the faster rabbits have a better chance of surviving, they live to reproduce and soon outnumber the slow rabbits, which frequently end up in the belly of a fox rather than creating offspring. By the end of the simulation, rabbits have evolved into speedy creatures that easily outfox foxes.

Peter Oppenheimer at the New York Institute of Technology wrote a program that uses the rules of evolution to create various types of computer trees. Each tree has 15 genes controlling its physical appearance, including the amount of twist in the branches and the color of the bark. Not willing to leave his trees to the vagaries of chance, however, Oppenheimer takes on the role of evolutionary influence, allowing only those trees he finds aesthetically pleasing to survive. For example, should Oppenheimer decide he prefers blue trees to red trees, the color blue becomes a survival trait, the same way speed is a survival trait for the rabbits in Jefferson's rabbit-and-fox program. This "artificial selection" combined with evolution soon yields trees with the characteristics Oppenheimer chose.

As computers grow more powerful, the simulations they can run become more complex. Before long, a-life simulations will be more intelligent and realistic, allowing the creation of more sophisticated organisms demonstrating a full array of lifelike behaviors, not simply a select few. Perhaps today, we feel comfortable saying a roach is living and a computer is not, but the time will surely come when we can no longer be so sure—a time when we'll have to recognize our bias toward traditional forms of life as a bias and nothing more.

The Game of Life

Now that you've read about the many a-life studies being conducted, it's time for you to conduct one of your own. In the next few pages, you learn more about Conway's famous Game of Life. You can even run the simulation yourself, but first you must install the program on your computer.

On this book's disk, you'll find two versions of Life: one for DOS users, written by your humble author; and one for Windows users, written by M. Zack Urlocker. The DOS version is called LIFE.EXE, and the Windows version is called PLIFE.EXE. To install either version, please refer to the installation instructions on the last page of this book (facing the disk).

You can play the Life simulation on a grid of any size. In the original rules the grid is unbounded, but you can limit it to the screen. In this case, you might want to think of the screen display as a petri dish holding a culture of microscopic cells. You place cells on the grid. When the simulation begins, the cells then run through their life cycles for a given number of generations, living and dying according to the rules set by Mr. Conway.

The rules are simple and elegant: Any live cell with fewer than two neighbors dies of loneliness. Any live cell with more than three neighbors dies of crowding. Any dead cell with exactly three neighbors comes to life. And, finally, any live cell with two or three neighbors lives, unchanged, to the next generation.

The DOS Version of Life

To run the DOS version of Life, change to the \ALIFE\LIFE directory, type **LIFE.EXE**, and press Enter. The main screen appears, as shown in Figure 2.8. Press Enter to close the welcome window, and you see that most of the screen comprises the grid in which your cells live and die.

Below the grid is the button bar containing several command buttons used to control the program. Also at the bottom of the screen, to the right, is the generation count. Before the simulation starts, this readout shows the current setting for the number of generations (the default is 100). As the simulation runs, the readout shows the number of the current generation.

To get started, you must first seed the grid with cells. To do this, place your mouse pointer where you want to place a cell and click the left button. A green cell appears where you clicked. If you want to place cells quickly, you can paint them onto the grid by holding down the left mouse button and sweeping the pointer across the screen. To seed cells from the keyboard, press Ctrl-R, which places a group of cells randomly in the grid. You can press Ctrl-R as often as you like to create a more dense population.

When you've placed your cells, activate the simulation by selecting the START button, either by clicking the button with your mouse or by pressing Ctrl-S. When you select START, the simulation springs

28

into life as cells start speeding through their life cycles. To stop the simulation before the generations run out, click the mouse or press any key.

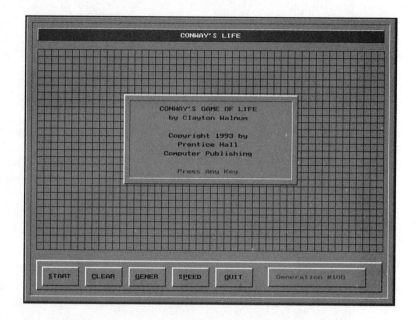

CONWAY'S LIFE

CONWAY'S GAME OF LIFE
by Clayton Walnum

Copyright 1993 by
Prentice Hall
Computer Publishing

Press Any Key

START   CLEAR   GENER   SPEED   QUIT   Generation #100

Figure 2.8.

The main screen of the DOS version of Conway's Game of Life.

Next to the START button is the CLEAR button, which removes all cells from the grid. The GENER button sets the generation count. When you select this button, the Generations dialog box appears, as shown in Figure 2.9. To change the generation setting, type a number from 1 to 10,000. Invalid entries yield the default value of 100.

You might want to view the simulation at slower speeds so you can see more clearly the patterns that emerge from specific cell configurations. You can set the simulation to one of 10 speeds by selecting the SPEED button. The Simulation Speed dialog box then appears, as shown in Figure 2.10. Enter a value from 1 to 10. (1 is the slowest and 10 is the fastest.) Invalid entries yield the default value of 10.

To quit the simulation, select the QUIT button. A Yes/No box appears, asking whether you really want to quit. Select Yes to exit the program or No to return to the simulation.

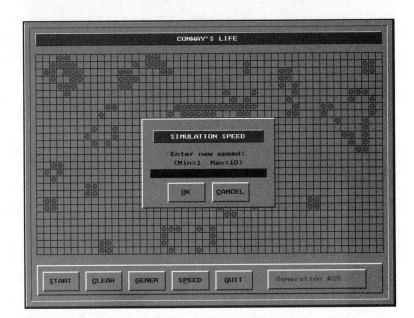

Figure 2.9.

*The Generations
dialog box.*

Figure 2.10.

*The Simulation
Speed dialog box.*

30

The Windows Version of Life (PLife)

The Windows version of the simulation, called PLife, is similar
to the DOS version. However, it must run from the Microsoft

Windows environment. If you don't have Windows, you cannot run this version of the Game of Life. After installing the program (see the last page of the book, facing the disk), run it by double-clicking the file PLIFE.EXE while in the File Manager. When the program first appears, you see the window shown in Figure 2.11.

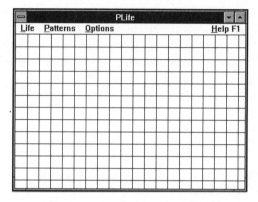

Figure 2.11.

The Windows version of Conway's Game of Life.

This version of the simulation, although similar to the DOS version, has some extra interesting options. For example, you can right-click inside the window, or simply press Ctrl-Z, to zoom in or out on the grid. For the best results, you might want to zoom back as far as possible, which gives you the largest amount of workspace. Also, you might want to click the window's maximize button to enlarge the grid to full size.

As with the DOS version of the Game of Life, you seed the grid by clicking your mouse. If you want to get started quickly (or if you don't have a mouse), you can choose the Random command on the Patterns menu to fill the grid with randomly placed cells. Select this command by clicking it or by pressing Ctrl-R. Other patterns you can choose are blooms and walkers. (See the section entitled "The Patterns of Life.") Choose the Bloom or Walker commands by clicking them or by pressing Ctrl-B or Ctrl-W, respectively.

Once you've seeded the grid with cells, start the simulation by selecting the Life menu's Go command or by pressing Ctrl-G. To stop the simulation, select the Life menu's Stop command or press Ctrl-S.

In this version of Life, you can add cells to the grid while the simulation runs, which enables you to stir up new activity when the action slows down. However, don't forget to turn off the simulation if you want to start over and reseed the grid. If you leave the simulation on, your cells die of loneliness as fast as you place them.

> **NOTE:** If you want to speed up or slow down the simulation, you can set the time between generations by selecting the Timer command of the Options menu, or by pressing Ctrl-M. The Timer Speed dialog box then appears, as shown in Figure 2.12. Type a new value and press Enter. The lower the timer value is, the faster the simulation runs.

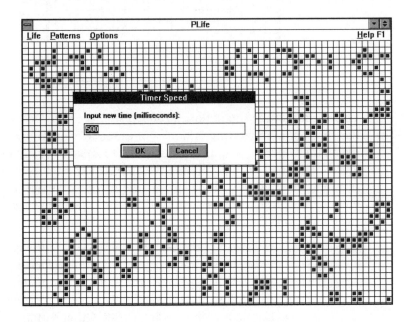

Figure 2.12.

The Timer Speed dialog box.

The Patterns of Life

As you tinker with the Game of Life, you'll notice that certain types of patterns tend to emerge. Often, your grid of cells hones itself down to a set of stable communities in which cells never come to life or die. Figure 2.13 shows some of these cell configurations.

Other communities settle in one place, but stay active by constantly changing between a set of fixed patterns. Figure 2.14 shows these types of communities.

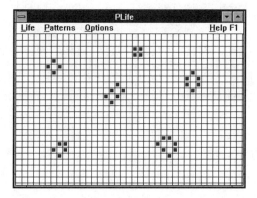

Figure 2.13.

Stable, inactive communities of cells.

Figure 2.14.

Stable, but still active, communities of cells.

Some patterns occur so often that they've been given names. The *spinners,* for example, are famous for their propeller type of activity. The *walkers* oscillate between different patterns, causing the community to migrate across the grid. Finally, the *bloom* is probably the most fascinating pattern of cells—it starts as a simple shape and then explodes into a kaleidoscopic display. When you place many blooms on-screen at a set distance from each other, you can receive breathtaking results, as shown in Figure 2.15.

Figure 2.15.

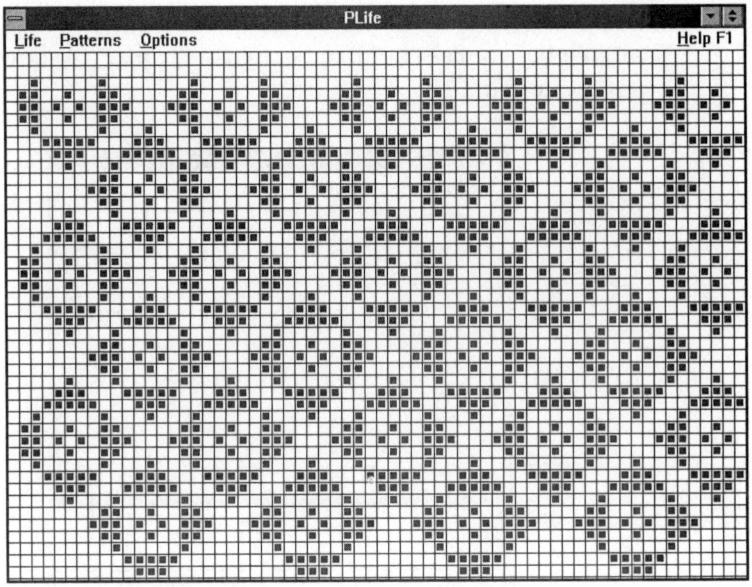

*Blooms generate
complex
kaleidoscopic
patterns.*

Conclusion

Although Conway's Game of Life is a simple simulation when
compared with the complex programs being developed today, it
demonstrates a biosphere in which single-celled creatures live and
die according to preset rules. As you've seen, the patterns that
emerge are often very lifelike. The rules used to control other a-life
simulations, however, are not as simple as those in Conway's
creation. In the next chapter, you learn how some of these more
complex programs work.

A View from Within: How A-Life Works

Now that you are familiar with artificial life and some of the experiments being conducted, it's time to see how these fascinating a-life programs work. Understanding the details of implementing a-life techniques requires a good knowledge of programming, but almost anybody can understand the general techniques.

In this chapter, you learn how a computer's memory can represent knowledge. Along the way, you see how a computer can simulate the human brain, how a simple program like Conway's Game of Life decides which cells should live and die, and how a computer program implements the basics of genetics by allowing artificial organisms to evolve.

Knowledge Representation in A-Life

Obviously, if a program is to simulate life on a computer screen, the computer has to "know" how to do this. The programmer must encode the behaviors that represent an artificial life form in a way the computer can understand. Then, once the computer has this knowledge, it can simply follow the instructions and generate as realistic a simulation as its knowledge base allows.

For example, suppose you're an a-life researcher and you are creating a computer program that simulates a roach. Because you're a wonderful programmer, creating the roach's graphical image is a snap. You even manage to animate the image so the roach scampers realistically around the screen. But so far, your roach is little more than a lot of colored dots. Except for movement, it exhibits few characteristics of life.

You decide next that your artificial roach must not only move around the screen, but also gather food and avoid obstacles. Further, you decide that the roach must learn from its mistakes. Therefore, when it bumps into an obstacle, it must learn how to get around the obstacle and be able to apply that knowledge the next time an obstacle blocks its path. Finally, when the roach discovers a cache of food, it must remember the food's location, so it can return when it gets hungry.

You have to add all these behaviors to your computer program so it knows what to do when the roach bumps into an obstacle or finds food. Moreover, the program must be clever enough to record instructions for the new behaviors the roach learns as it wanders in its tiny digital world. The way the computer stores the roach's brain is called *knowledge representation*.

There are many ways to represent knowledge in a computer program. At the simplest level are *rule-based systems,* which are little more than many IF-THEN conditions and responses (for example, IF the roach is hungry, THEN it eats). At the high end are intricate *neural networks,* which represent knowledge in much the same way as the human brain does. (Debate continues over whether neural networks actually mimic the functions of the brain, but neural networks are at least modeled after the way scientists suspect the brain works.) You will start your examination of knowledge representation in a-life programs with rule-based systems.

Rule-Based Systems

A rule-based system is perhaps the easiest way to represent knowledge in a computer. In most computer programming languages, you implement a rule-based system using IF-THEN instructions, which match specific conditions to specific actions. In the roach program, for example, you might write a computer instruction that states, "If the roach bumps into an obstacle, turn the roach 15 degrees to the right." Similarly, you might have an IF-THEN instruction that states, "If the roach steps onto a food square, make the roach eat."

Using many such rules, a computer program can represent myriad lifelike behaviors. Your roach can walk around the screen, turning away from obstacles when it encounters them and stopping to eat when it discovers food. You can even add a simple reproductive rule that states if the roach eats a certain amount of food, it must divide into two roaches.

The trouble with the rule-based approach is that the roach has no way to learn new behaviors. If you want the roach to do something new, you must stop the program and add instructions that will implement the new behavior. Your roach simulation is little more than an on-screen robot, like those electronic toys that change their direction when they bump into walls. The roach has all its abilities when the simulation begins, and its experiences have no effect on its future behavior.

Finite-State Automata

Another way you can represent knowledge in a computer is with *finite-state automata* (pronounced aw-TOM-a-ta). This is a fancy name for a table of states. An object begins with a predefined state and moves from one state to another according to the entries of a state-transition table.

For example, you can represent your roach's behavior as the finite-state automaton shown in Figure 3.1. You can say that walking is State #1, turning is State #2, and eating is State #3. To start the simulation, you place the roach in State #1. Your program sees that the roach is in State #1 and starts the roach walking across the screen. Then, when some stimulus—such as bumping into a wall—requires the roach to react, your program examines the state-transition table to determine the roach's new state.

	Struck Wall	Found Food	Avoided Wall	Hunger Satiated
State #1 (Walking)	2	3	X	X
State #2 (Turning)	2	3	1	X
State #3 (Eating)	X	X	X	1

Figure 3.1.

Finite-state automata employ a state-transition table to translate a stimulus into a new state.

Assume the roach is walking, and it bumps into a wall. The program checks the square at the intersection of the current state (State #1) and the current stimulus (Struck Wall). The new state becomes State #2, Turning, so the program begins turning the roach. By consulting the table, the program knows that the roach keeps turning as long as it is in State #2 and is hitting a wall (as shown at the intersection of State #2 and Struck Wall). However, as soon as the wall is gone, the roach reverts to State #1, Walking, as shown at the intersection of State #2 and the stimulus, Avoided Wall.

Now that the roach is back in State #1, suppose it finds a cache of food. Checking the state-transition table where State #1 intersects with Found Food, the program knows that the roach's new state is State #3, Eating. Likewise, when the roach has had its fill, it reverts to State #1, Walking, as shown at the intersection of State #3 and Hunger Satiated.

Not all state/stimulus combinations produce a new state. For example, when the roach is eating, it's not possible for it to hit a wall, find new food, or avoid a wall. Table entries that don't apply to the current state are marked with Xs, which indicate undefined states.

You can easily implement Conway's Game of Life using a finite-state automaton. (Conway's Game of Life is also an example of a cellular automata, which is a grid of cells whose states depend upon the states of neighboring cells. A great deal of research in a-life is done with cellular automata.) Figure 3.2 shows the resulting state-transition table. On the left side of the table are a cell's possible states (Alive or Dead). Across the top of the table are the possible stimuli. In this case, the stimuli are the cell's neighbor counts.

To check for a cell's new state, find the current state on the left side of the table and follow it across to the column representing the new stimulus. For example, if the current state is State #1, Alive, and the neighbor count is four, the cell's new state is State #2, Dead. Similarly, if the cell's current state is State #2, Dead and the neighbor count is three, the cell's new state is State #1, Alive.

NUMBER OF NEIGHBORS

	One	Two	Three	> Three
State #1 (Alive)	2	1	1	2
State #2 (Dead)	2	2	1	2

Figure 3.2.

You can represent Conway's Game of Life as a finite-state automaton.

Unfortunately, although a finite-state automaton is a handy way to represent knowledge in a computer, it suffers the same problems as a rule-based system. It does not allow for new behavior unless the programmer adds new states and stimuli to the state-transition table. One way to overcome this limitation is to use a *neural network*.

Neural Networks

The human brain is a huge mass of cells connected in a network so incredibly complex it defies description. Each of these cells, called *neurons,* gather input from other cells to which they're connected and generate output based on the strengths of the inputs. Figure 3.3 shows how a neuron is constructed. The dendrites gather signals from other neurons. When these signals are of sufficient strength, they cause the neuron to "fire," which sends a pulse from the cell's

body, down the axon, and out into the synapse, which is the connection to the following neurons.

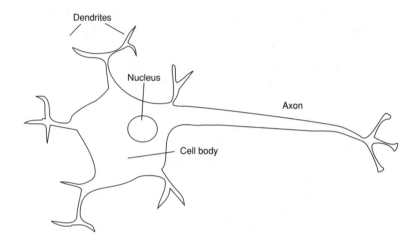

Dendrites

Nucleus

Axon

Cell body

Figure 3.3.

The brain comprises billions of neurons, which are interconnected into a complex network.

Scientists have studied long and hard to understand how the billions and billions of neurons in the brain stimulate learning. In the course of their studies, computer scientists have attempted to duplicate neurons on computers. These neural simulations, called neural networks, not only help scientists understand the secret workings of the brain, but also enable them to create computer applications that learn.

On a computer, a neural network comprises many nodes, each of which represents a single neuron. Each node is connected to other nodes in much the same way neurons in the brain are connected. Figure 3.4 provides a visualization of how neurons are represented in a computer. Each input value to the node is processed by multiplying the input by a weighting factor. The results of all a node's inputs are then totaled, and if the sum is greater than the node's threshold, the node fires, sending input to the next nodes in the network. In a simple neural network, the output of a node is 1 if it fires and 0 if it does not fire.

Neural networks incorporate three layers of nodes, as shown in Figure 3.5. The first nodes represent the *input layer*—the source of the network's input. The signals from the input layer are processed and passed to the *hidden layer,* which further processes the input and passes the results to the *output layer*. The output generated by the output layer is the network's result.

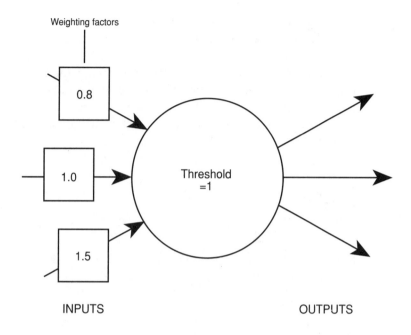

Weighting factors

0.8

1.0

Threshold
=1

1.5

INPUTS

OUTPUTS

Figure 3.4.

A node in a neural network. The input values are multiplied by their weighting factors and then summed. If the total input is higher than the node's threshold value, the node fires.

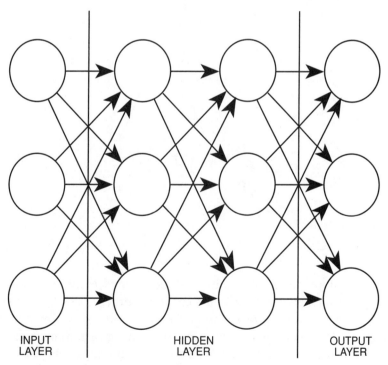

INPUT
LAYER

HIDDEN
LAYER

OUTPUT
LAYER

Figure 3.5.

Neural networks comprise input nodes, hidden nodes, and output nodes.

Figure 3.6 shows how a neural network can determine whether two animals are of the same family. The animals' names are represented by the network's input layer. The input layer is connected to the hidden layer by a series of connections, each of which has a weighting factor of 1. (The weighting factors are shown in boxes on each connection.) Similarly, the hidden layer connects to the output layer, except these connections have weighting factors of either 1 or –1.

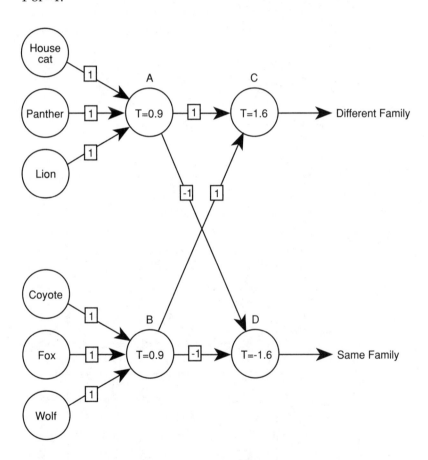

Suppose you feed "house cat" and "panther" into the network, which activates the house cat and panther nodes. These nodes each output a value of 1. The hidden node A receives a total input of 2, which you can determine by multiplying each individual input times the weighting factor, and then summing the results. Node A's

threshold is 0.9, so this input of 2 causes node A to fire, sending a value of 1 down its connections to nodes C and D. (*Remember: The values shown in the boxes are the connections' weighting factors, not the values coming from node A.*) Figure 3.7A summarizes this process.

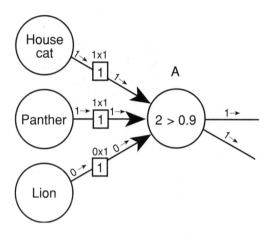

Figure 3.7A.

When the house cat and panther nodes fire, the node to which they're connected also fires.

Meanwhile, at the second set of input nodes—coyote, fox, and wolf—no input connections are active, so each outputs a value of 0. The total input to hidden node B, then, is also 0. Because the total input of 0 is not higher than the node's threshold of 0.9, the node does not fire, which means node B's output is 0, as shown in Figure 3.7B.

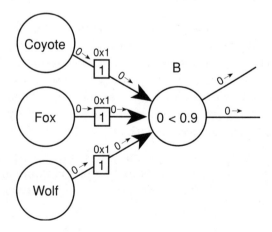

Figure 3.7B.

The coyote, fox, and wolf nodes have not fired, so node B doesn't fire either.

43

Now, node C receives a total input of 1 and does not fire, because 1 is not greater than its threshold of 1.6. Node D, though, receives a total input of –1, which is larger than node D's threshold of –1.6. Node D fires, which tells you that both animals are members of the same family. Figure 3.7C summarizes this final process.

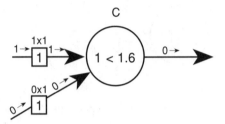

Figure 3.7C.

Thanks to the connections' weighting factors, only node D fires, indicating that a house cat and panther are in the same family of animals.

Now, suppose the panther and wolf input nodes are active. Use what you've learned about neural networks to trace a path through the network. If you do it correctly, you should wind up at the output of node C.

You can see how, by following a path through the connections in the network, you can translate an input into a correct output. However, in this example, no learning has taken place. You already know how to set up the connections between the nodes to produce the result you want. But suppose you have a "blank" neural network, one with connections that are not properly weighted so they produce the desired output?

Neural networks are powerful objects in a-life because they can weigh their own connections. The program provides sample input to the network, then compares the output of the network with the

desired result. If the result is incorrect, the weights on the connections are modified (using fancy calculations beyond the scope of this book) in such a way that the output result becomes closer to the desired result. By changing each connection's weighting factor, a neural network modifies the route a signal takes through the network. By providing many input samples and modifying the network for each input, one eventually teaches the network to produce correct results.

Genetic Algorithms

In the real world, the process of natural selection controls evolution. Organisms most suited for their environment tend to live long enough to reproduce, whereas less-suited organisms die before producing young. In a-life simulations, scientists can study the process of evolution by creating an artificial world, populating it with organisms, and giving those organisms a goal to achieve. Using genetic algorithms, the scientists can teach the organisms to achieve their goal through a crude form of evolution.

What's a genetic algorithm? An algorithm is simply a series of steps for solving a problem. A *genetic algorithm,* then, is a problem-solving method that uses genetics as its model. In short, genetic algorithms apply the rules of reproduction, gene crossover, and mutation to artificial organisms so those organisms can pass traits to a new generation.

How Can a Neural Network Be Applied to an A-Life Simulation?

Suppose you take your roach and give it an untrained neural network for a brain. As the roach wanders around the screen, it runs into situations that it must learn to handle. As the programmer, you know that when the roach bumps into a wall, it must turn away. So, when the roach crashes into a wall, the program sends collision information into the network. If the network's output indicates an action other than turning, the result is incorrect.

The roach performs the incorrect behavior because it doesn't yet know any better. To simulate the roach's new experience, however, the program modifies the weighting factors of the network's connections so the next time the roach bumps into a wall, the network's output is closer to what it's supposed to be. Eventually, the roach learns exactly what to do when it hits the wall, and, in this way, learns its own rules of behavior.

Artificial Genotypes

In the real world, an organism's characteristics are encoded in its DNA. Genetic algorithms store the characteristics of artificial organisms in an *electronic genotype,* which mimics the DNA of natural life. This electronic genotype is nothing more than a long string of bits. As mentioned in Chapter 2, a bit is the smallest piece of data a computer can process. It can be only one of two values: 0 or 1. When a bit in the genotype string is "on" (has the value 1), a certain characteristic is apparent in the artificial organism. When a bit is "off" (has the value of 0), that characteristic is missing. Because some behaviors might be too complex to be represented by a single on or off switch, many bits are often considered together as a unit or gene.

For example, a program can represent only two states with a single bit (0 or 1). If the bit is to represent a movement pattern, only two types of movement are allowed. To implement four types of movement requires two bits, which can take on four distinct patterns: 00, 10, 01, and 11.

In an a-life simulation, creatures start with randomly generated genotypes. Defective creatures are unable to attain their assigned goal and die off quickly, whereas creatures with advantageous genotypes survive and reproduce, passing their genetic material to their offspring.

To start designing a simulation, the programmer has to design the genotype by deciding which bits represent which behaviors. For example, suppose a programmer creates a four-bit gene. He decides that the first two bits determine how the creature moves, with 00 indicating no movement, 01 indicating straight-line movement, 10 (pronounced "one zero," not "ten") indicating zig-zag movement, and 11 (pronounced "one one," not "eleven") indicating circular movement. He might further decide that bit 3 determines whether a creature can recognize an enemy (1 if yes, 0 if no) and bit 4 determines whether a creature tries to fight an enemy (1) or runs away when attacked (0). Figure 3.8 illustrates this genotype.

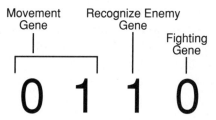

Movement Gene   Recognize Enemy Gene   Fighting Gene

0 1 1 0

Figure 3.8.

Bits in an artificial genotype represent the behaviors exhibited in an artificial life form.

Populating the Artificial World

Now that the programmer has designed her genotype, she must create a starting population. Suppose she decides that her computerized world will start with five creatures. The programmer then randomly generates five genotypes, one for each creature. Whether a particular bit in a genotype is on or off is determined by a type of electronic coin toss. The programmer might end up with the creatures in Table 3.1.

Table 3.1. Five randomly generated genotypes.

Creature Number	Genotype
1	0110
2	1011
3	0001
4	1100
5	1111

Looking at the genotype for creature 1 and comparing it with Figure 3.8, you can see that the creature moves in a straight line, recognizes enemies, and runs from a fight. Creature 2, on the other hand, moves in a zig-zag pattern, recognizes an enemy, and fights when attacked. Depending on how the programmer sets up the artificial world in which the creatures live, some of these genes prove to be beneficial, whereas others lead only to death.

Suppose, for example, the programmer decides that his creatures' enemies will be good fighters but slow runners. This means that creatures with the gene for running from a fight have a better chance of survival. On the other hand, if the enemies are fast runners, there's no advantage to a creature running, because the enemy will catch it anyway.

Achieving a Goal Means Survival

Next, the programmer must decide on a goal for her creatures. Perhaps they have to eat a certain amount of food to reproduce. Obviously then, a creature must survive long enough to eat the food. Those creatures that survive pass their advantaged genotypes to their offspring. Genetically disadvantaged creatures don't generally live long enough to reproduce, which means their genotypes will eventually vanish from the genetic pool.

When the simulation runs, creatures are scored on how well they attain their goal. For example, if the goal is finding food, the creatures that eat the most food best achieve their goal. Once a creature eats a certain predetermined amount of food, it reproduces, thus passing its successful genes to another generation.

Employing Crossover in Reproduction

In a simple simulation, creatures reproduce asexually. That is, like most one-celled animals, they simply produce an exact copy of themselves. However, for a more realistic simulation, you can employ sexual reproduction, which causes the genotypes from two creatures to be merged into new genotypes for the offspring.

Crossover determines what parts of the parents' genotypes appear in the offsprings' genotypes. Often, the program randomly calculates a *crossover site,* which determines the border between one parent's genetic contribution and the other's, as shown in Figure 3.9. Employing crossover slows the evolutionary process, because, although mating two creatures with advantageous genotypes usually yields superior offspring, mating a superior organism to a weak one yields weaker offspring. In a properly constructed simulation, however, the end result should be the same, with the weaker genotypes disappearing, leaving only superior parents to produce superior offspring.

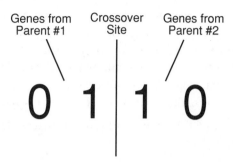

Genes from Parent #1   Crossover Site   Genes from Parent #2

0 1 1 0

Figure 3.9.

The crossover site is the border between parents' genetic contributions.

Mutation as an Evolutionary Factor

Mutation is another factor that affects evolution in the real world. When creatures reproduce, there's no guarantee the resulting genotype will be reproduced perfectly. Often, reproduction introduces unpredictable changes to the genotype, creating new characteristics that may or may not be advantageous. Those creatures with positive mutations tend to live to reproduce. Those with negative mutations die off.

In genetic algorithms, mutation is introduced by changing a randomly determined bit in the genotype. The programmer programs this change to occur according to a percentage chance. For example, a programmer might determine that mutation is to occur once for every 100 matings, which means about one percent of all offspring will contain a *defective* gene. (One might question the word defective because the change introduced by mutation might very well turn out to be a positive one.)

Neural Networks and Genetic Algorithms in Action

The book's disk contains two programs that demonstrate some of the a-life programming techniques presented in this chapter. The first program, called Nervous System Construction Kit, uses a neural network to simulate the behavior of a roach—a roach not unlike the little fellow you read about earlier.

The second program, MicroAnts, uses genetic algorithms to simulate the evolution of a colony of ants. These ants have genes for controlling how well they see, how they move, whether they can recognize poison, when they mate, and whether they share food with other ants. By varying the amount of food and poison in the ant's world, you can cause different types of ants to evolve.

Take a look at the Nervous System Construction Kit first.

Experimenting with Neural Networks

At Case Western Reserve University, Dr. Randall Beer and his colleagues study life by attempting to re-create a common cockroach on a computer. Using a sophisticated neural network comprising 78 neurons and 156 connections, Beer taught his artificial insect (called *Periplaneta computatrix*) to walk, navigate around obstacles, and search out and eat food.

What's amazing about Beer's roach is not so much what it can do, but how it goes about doing it. When P. computatrix walks, for example, it duplicates the gaits of a real cockroach. Just as a horse walks, trots, and gallops—each gait having its own distinctive pattern of leg movement—so P. computatrix performs metachronal waves and tripod gaits, patterns of leg movement observed in actual roaches. Surprisingly, not all the observed gaits are programmed, but rather occur due to the complex interaction of the 38 neurons that control the roach's movement.

Each leg is controlled by its own group of six neurons. Three motor neurons control the foot, the force of the forward swing, and the force of the backward swing. In addition, a pacemaker neuron and two sensory neurons work together to maintain the proper walking rhythm. Finally, two command neurons control the overall activity of all six legs.

P. computatrix also sports neurons that allow it to turn as it walks, to follow the edges of obstacles, and to eat. In addition, the artificial roach is equipped with a series of sensors that enable it to detect changes in its body and environment. The mouth, for example, features tactile and chemical sensors to help it find food. The antennae, too, have chemical sensors, although with a longer range, as well as sensors that can sense contact with objects. The legs each have sensors that inform the insect when a leg is fully extended

forward or backward. Finally, P. computatrix has internal sensors that monitor its energy level.

Pat and Greg Williams of Kentucky were so fascinated with Beer's work that they set about writing their own version of P. compu-tatrix. The results of their labor, the Nervous System Construction Kit (NSCK), is on this book's disk—file name NS.EXE. (Please see the last page of the book—facing the disk—for installation instructions.) Although the details of this complex program are beyond the scope of this discussion, you can run the program and see the roach in action. You can even manipulate its environment as you observe this remarkable example of a-life.

Running the Nervous System Construction Kit

To run NSCK, change to the \ALIFE\ROACH directory and type **NS.EXE**. The program's main menu appears on your screen, as shown in Figure 3.10. To function, NSCK requires that you load two data files. The first, a neuron file, contains the details of neural network circuitry. The second, the environment file, contains the objects in the simulation's on-screen world, including obstacles and food patches.

```
Read files

Write files

Neuron data modification

Environment specification

Initialize conditions

Graph specification

Path specification for recording

Simulate

Quit
```

Figure 3.10.

The Nervous System Construc-tion Kit's main menu.

To load one set of sample files for NSCK, follow these instructions:

1. From the main menu, press R to choose the Read files option.

2. Type **APP3.NEU** and press Enter.

3. Type **APP3.ENV** and press Enter.

These two files provide the simulated roach with wandering, edge-following, and eating behaviors, as well as a world containing a single obstacle and food patch. Other data sets on the disk include the WANDER.NEU and WANDER.ENV files, which demonstrate only the roach's wandering behavior, and the EDGE3.NEU and EDGE3.ENV, which demonstrate both wandering and edge-following behaviors.

P. Computatrix in Action

When you've loaded the data files, you're ready to see the roach explore its new world. From the main menu, press S to switch to the simulation screen, which is shown in Figure 3.11. Then press Enter to nudge the roach into action.

How the roach behaves on your screen is controlled not only by its neural network, but also by what it encounters as it wanders. For example, if the roach turns to the north and starts following the edge of the screen, it might never become aware of the food patch and might follow the edge until it starves. On the other hand, if the roach turns to the south and finds its way around the center obstacle, it'll almost certainly sense the food patch, move to it, and eat it.

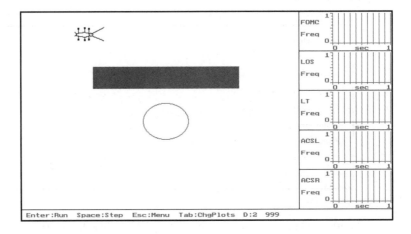

Figure 3.11.

The simulation's main screen.

The graphs to the right of the main display show the activity of a few of the roach's neurons. To see how complex the interaction between the neurons is, follow these instructions:

1. Press the Spacebar to enter the simulation's step mode.

2. Press Tab to switch off the graph display.

3. Press Enter to exit step mode.

When the roach starts moving again, a list of its neurons appears where the graphs were, as shown in Figure 3.12. Dark blue neurons are inactive. Other neurons are firing. As you can see by the neurons' rapid blinking, a lot is going on under this little fellow's carapace.

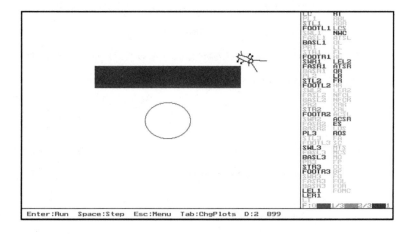

Enter:Run   Space:Step   Esc:Menu   Tab:ChgPlots   D:2   899

Figure 3.12.

The main screen with the neuron list having replaced the graph display.

Unfortunately, displaying the neuron list slows the simulation considerably, so you'll probably want to switch back to the graph display. To do this, press the Spacebar to enter step mode, press Tab to redisplay the graphs, and then press Enter to restart the simulation.

Modifying the Simulation

If you're unhappy with the roach's current antics, you can change its behavior by modifying its conditions, as follows:

1. Press Escape to return to the main menu.

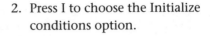

Your Own Experiment

As an experiment, try giving the roach an energy level of 999, which represents a full belly, and positioning it near the food patch. Because the roach is satiated, it should ignore the food. Then reduce its energy to 300 and position it near the food. Now the roach should eat.

2. Press I to choose the Initialize conditions option.

3. Type a new value for the roach's X coordinate (horizontal position), and press Enter.

4. Type a new value for the roach's Y coordinate (vertical position), and press Enter.

5. Type a new value for the roach's angle, and press Enter.

6. Type a new value for the roach's energy level, and press Enter.

7. Press S to return to the main screen.

8. Press Enter to start the simulation with the new conditions.

If you want to modify the roach's environment, follow these instructions:

1. Press Escape to return to the main menu.

2. Press E to select the Environment specification option.

3. Type the number of food patches you want and press Enter.

4. Type the position and size of each food patch, pressing Enter after each value.

5. Type the number of obstacles and press Enter.

6. Type the position of each obstacle, pressing Enter after each entry.

7. Press S to return to the main screen.

8. Press Enter to start the simulation.

Experiment with different setups to see how the roach reacts. You might, for example, construct a maze the roach must navigate to find food. If you create an environment you want to keep, use the following instructions to save the environment to your disk:

1. Return to the main menu and press W to select the Write files option.

2. When asked whether you want to save a neuron file, press N. (The neural network is too complicated to risk changing unless you really know what you are doing.)

3. When asked whether to save an environment file, press Y.

4. When asked whether to save the file to APP3.ENV (or what-ever file you have currently loaded), press N, unless you want to erase the original file.

5. When prompted, type the new file name (for example, **MYENV.ENV**) for the environment, and press Enter.

After saving a new environment file, you can reload it at any time using the Read files menu option.

Recording the Simulation

Because the simulation runs slowly, you might want to record it for later playback at higher speeds. To record the simulation while it's running, press any of the function keys (F1-F10) on your keyboard. The simulation is saved to a file called NSx.SAV, in which x is the number of the F key you pressed. To stop the recording, press Escape.

Once you create a recording, you can play it back using the NSPLAY.EXE program, which you will find in the same directory as NS.EXE. To run the program, type **NSPLAY**, followed by the name of the file containing the recorded simulation, and press Enter. When the simulation starts playing, you can change the speed by first pressing the Spacebar to enter single-step mode, and then pressing the – or + keys (on the numeric keypad) to slow or speed the playback.

The Nervous System Construction Kit contains several menu options not mentioned previously. The Path specification for recording option enables you to change where you store recorded simulations. Although it's sensible to save your data into the same directory as the program, feel free to change the path if you like.

The remaining options are not for the faint of heart. The Graph specification option enables you to change which neurons are shown in the graphs on the main screen. Obviously, unless you know what all the neurons do, this option doesn't help you much. Similarly, the Neuron data modification option enables you to modify the characteristics of the neural network (which is why the program is called the Nervous System Construction Kit). However, unless you are familiar with Dr. Beer's work and the way he constructed his neural network, you'll find this task overwhelming, to say the least.

NOTE: If you are interested in learning more about NSCK, Dr. Beer has published a book entitled *Intelligence as Adaptive Behavior: An Experiment in Computational Neuroethology* (Academic Press) that describes Beer's bug model in detail. Pat and Greg Williams, the authors of NSCK, strongly recommend that anyone interested in fully understanding NSCK should read Dr. Beer's book.

Experimenting with Genetic Algorithms

Although the Nervous System Construction Kit is an involved program that assumes an intimate knowledge of the work on which it's based, MicroAnts, programmed by Steve Wright, is a simpler a-life example. MicroAnts clearly demonstrates the use of genetic algorithms to simulate evolution.

To run the program, move to the \ALIFE\ANTS directory and type **ANTS.EXE**. When the title screen appears, press Enter. The program then asks for the parameters it needs to start the simulation, as shown in Figure 3.13.

Understanding MicroAnts' Parameters

Before entering MicroAnts' parameters, look over the list that follows to see what each value means.

- *Number of Ants:* The starting population of the simulation. Each ant starts at a random location on-screen and begins life with a randomly generated genotype.

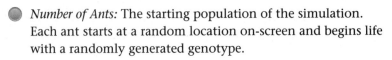

● *Initial Number of Food:* The number of randomly placed food units with which the simulation starts.

● *Number of Food Grown in One Year:* The number of food units that should be added to the screen in each simulation cycle. To keep the number of food units constant, use 999, which makes one unit grow for each unit eaten.

● *Maximum Number of Food:* The maximum number of food units allowed on-screen simultaneously.

● *Number of Poison:* The number of randomly placed poison units with which the simulation begins.

● *Average Number of Crossovers:* The average percentage of crossovers that occur during mating. A value of 25, for example, makes an average of 25 percent of the new genotypes combinations of two parent genotypes.

● *Average Number of Mutations:* The average number of mutations that occur per every 10 matings.

● *Speed of Simulation:* How fast the simulation runs.

```
                    MicroAnts Environment Setup


Number of Ants --> 300

Initial Number of Food --> 30

Number of Food Grown in One Year (999 for 1 eaten, 1 grown) --> 3

Maximum Number of Food --> 300

Number of Poison --> 1

Average number of crossovers per 1 hundred matings (0..100) --> 15

Average number of mutations per 1 hundred alleles (0..100) --> 5

Speed of simulation: [F]ast or [S]low (press 'f' or 's' to choose).
```

Figure 3.13.

*MicroAnts'
parameter entry
screen.*

To keep things simple at first, enter the following values for the program's starting parameters:

Number of Ants: 30
Initial Food: 300
Food Grown: 999

Maximum Food: 300
Number of Poison: 0
Crossover Rate: 15
Mutation Rate: 4
Simulation Speed: F

The Statistics Screen

When you enter the parameters, the program creates the simulated world, after which MicroAnts' main menu appears, as shown in Figure 3.14. Press A to view your new ants' statistics. The statistics screen, shown in Figure 3.15, then appears.

```
                           MicroAnts Main Menu




                              Do you wish to:



        View [A]nt Statistics,
        View [B]est Ant Hall of Fame,
        [C]olor an Ant,
        Run the Simulation and [P]ause After Each Year,
        [R]un the Simulation (pressing any key returns to the Main Menu),
        Change the [S]peed of the Simulation,
        View [U]niverse Statistics, or
        [Q]uit.




              Please press the key corresponding to your choice.
```

Figure 3.14.

MicroAnts' main menu.

Figure 3.15.

MicroAnts' statistics screen.

#	ID#	Food	Age	Matings	Sharings	Chromosome	Gen	Parent1	Parent2
1	1	50	0	0	0	1100110000	0	0	0
2	2	50	0	0	0	1101000111	0	0	0
3	3	50	0	0	0	1100011101	0	0	0
4	4	50	0	0	0	1110000110	0	0	0
5	5	50	0	0	0	1010110110	0	0	0
6	6	50	0	0	0	1110110001	0	0	0
7	7	50	0	0	0	0100100110	0	0	0
8	8	50	0	0	0	0101001000	0	0	0
9	9	50	0	0	0	0001010100	0	0	0
10	10	50	0	0	0	1110010100	0	0	0
11	11	50	0	0	0	1101010100	0	0	0
12	12	50	0	0	0	0011111010	0	0	0
13	13	50	0	0	0	1100000101	0	0	0
14	14	50	0	0	0	0010100110	0	0	0
15	15	50	0	0	0	1110010101	0	0	0
16	16	50	0	0	0	1001111001	0	0	0
17	17	50	0	0	0	0100010001	0	0	0
18	18	50	0	0	0	1111000101	0	0	0
19	19	50	0	0	0	0100001101	0	0	0
20	20	50	0	0	0	1110110000	0	0	0
21	21	50	0	0	0	0101001001	0	0	0
22	22	50	0	0	0	1101011111	0	0	0
23	23	50	0	0	0	0001111000	0	0	0
24	24	50	0	0	0	0111100100	0	0	0
25	25	50	0	0	0	0000100011	0	0	0
26	26	50	0	0	0	0001011001	0	0	0
27	27	50	0	0	0	0110111101	0	0	0
28	28	50	0	0	0	1010101101	0	0	0
29	29	50	0	0	0	0010100101	0	0	0
30	30	50	0	0	0	1010000001	0	0	0

Press Any Key to Return to the Main Menu

As you can see, each ant has its own set of statistics. The statistics are

ID#: A unique ID number for each ant.

Food: The ant's current energy level, that is, the number of food units the ant has eaten but not yet burned off. When this value reaches 0, the ant dies of starvation.

Age: The number of simulation cycles the ant has lived.

Matings: The number of times the ant has mated.

Sharings: The number of times the ant has shared food.

Chromosome: The ant's genotype.

Gen: The ant's generation number. New ants start at generation 0, and subsequent matings increase the generation number of the offspring.

Parent1 and Parent2: The ant's parents.

Because your ants are new, most of their statistics are 0, except for their food level, which begins at 50; their genotypes, which were randomly generated; and, of course, their ID numbers.

An Ant's Genotype

While you're on the statistics screen, examine your ants' genotypes. The genotypes used in MicroAnts are a bit more complicated than the four-bit genotype used with the roach example. These ants have genes that control how well they see, how they move, whether they can recognize poison, when they mate, and whether they'll share food with other ants. Each of these characteristics is based on the bit patterns, or genes, in an ant's genotype, as shown in Figure 3.16.

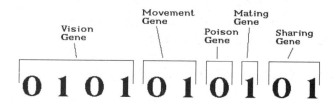

Figure 3.16.

The genotype used in MicroAnts.

You should interpret the genotype as follows:

Vision Gene: Determines how far an ant can see.

    0000 = Blind   1000 = 8 spaces
    0001 = 1 space   1001 = 9 spaces
    0010 = 2 spaces   1010 = 10 spaces
    0011 = 3 spaces   1011 = 11 spaces
    0100 = 4 spaces   1100 = 12 spaces
    0101 = 5 spaces   1101 = 13 spaces
    0110 = 6 spaces   1110 = 14 spaces
    0111 = 7 spaces   1111 = 15 spaces

Movement Gene: Determines the ant's movement pattern.

    00 = No movement
    01 = Moves up and down
    10 = Moves right and left
    11 = Moves in random directions

Poison Gene: Determines whether an ant will eat poison.

    0 = Will eat poison
    1 = Will not eat poison

Mating Gene: Determines the food level required to mate.

    0 = Mate when level is greater than 500
    1 = Mate when level is greater than 1000

Sharing Gene: Determines how an ant shares food.

    00 = Never shares food
    01 = Always shares food
    10 = Shares when other ant's bits 9 and 10 are the bit pattern 10 (one, zero)
    11 = Shares when other ant's bits 9 and 10 are the bit patterns 01 (zero, one) or 11 (one, one)

By examining the genotypes for your new ants, you can see that the starting bit patterns are completely random. When you start the simulation, however, ants begin searching for food, living or dying based on how well they attain that goal.

Your Living Colony

Press any key to exit the statistics screen, and then press R to start the simulation. When you do, the screen shown in Figure 3.17 appears. On-screen, your ants, represented by red circles (the darker circles), scamper about wildly, gobbling up food, represented by green circles. As you watch the ants, you'll notice that those with the best vision zero in on food quickly, whereas ants with poor vision wander aimlessly until they die.

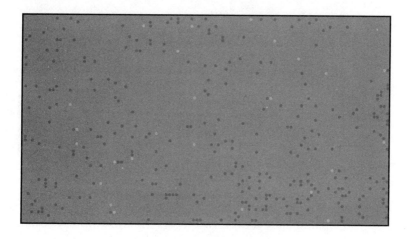

Figure 3.17.

MicroAnts' main simulation screen.

Let the program run for a while (five minutes or so), and then check the statistics screen. You'll discover that most ants now have pretty good vision. In fact, theoretically, the longer you let the program run, the better your ants' vision should become. To set up tougher competition between the ants, try running the simulation with a smaller amount of food...maybe 90 instead of 100.

The less food you plant, the better vision the ants must have to survive. However, with too little food, your ants die regardless of their genes. Also, keep in mind that their movement pattern, as well as their vision acuity, affects their ability to find food. Finally, their mating gene controls how often they can pass their genes to offspring. As you can see, even with only a few variables, the simulation becomes quite involved.

The Hall of Fame

After the simulation runs for a while, you might want to see which ants are doing the best overall job. To find this information, press Escape to return to the main menu, and then press B to see the *Ant Hall of Fame,* as shown in Figure 3.18.

GREATEST AGE				MOST FOOD		
Age	ID	Food	Chromosome	Food	ID	Chromosome
3108	1	1310	1100110000	4747	11	1110110100
3108	3	760	1100011101	3726	31	1110110100
3108	4	649	1110000110	3043	24	0111100100
3108	5	1011	1010110110	2956	38	1110111100
3108	6	981	1110110001	1802	45	0110110000
3108	7	864	0100100110	1775	10	1110010100
3108	10	1775	1110010100	1642	54	1010110110
3108	11	4747	1110110100	1638	34	0110110000
3108	14	514	0010100110	1463	59	1110110100
3108	15	805	1110010101	1438	58	1110010100

MOST MATINGS				MOST SHARINGS			
Matings	ID	Food	Chromosome	Sharings	ID	Food	Chromosome
10	20	229	1110110000	9	6	981	1110110001
8	1	1310	1100110000	9	15	805	1110010101
8	5	1011	1010110110	9	28	630	1010101101
8	10	1775	1110010100	8	50	1026	1101011111
7	7	864	0100100110	7	3	760	1100011101
6	6	981	1110110001	6	46	0 (Dead)	0110110001
6	16	793	1001111001	6	42	518	1110110001
6	37	927	1110010100	6	57	691	1111100101
5	3	760	1100011101	6	60	599	1001010001
5	15	805	1110010101	6	63	1060	1110110001

Press Any Key to Return to the Main Menu

Figure 3.18.

MicroAnts' Ant Hall of Fame screen.

The Hall of Fame is divided into four sections. Section one shows the oldest ants, section two shows the ants who have eaten the most food, section three shows the ants who have mated most often, and section four shows the ants who have shared food most often. When viewing this screen, examine the ants' *genotypes* (or *chromosomes,* as this program's author refers to them) to see whether you can tell why a particular ant made the Hall of Fame in a particular category.

NOTE: Remember that chance plays a critical part in an ant's survival. An ant with poor sight might survive simply because it's lucky enough to have food continually appearing close by. Still, the longer the simulation runs, the less effect chance has on the evolution of your ants. In the long run, an ant with poor sight has little chance of evolving into a dominant life form. In fact, this visually impaired friend is virtually guaranteed of extinction.

Tracking a Specific Ant

If you see an ant with a particularly interesting genotype, you can track it on-screen by changing its color to white, as follows:

1. Determine the ant's ID number from the statistics screen.

2. Press Escape to return to the main menu screen.

3. Press C to select the Color an Ant option.

4. Type the ant's ID number and press Enter.

When you return to the simulation screen, your ant is white, which makes it easier to follow.

Your Own Experiment

As an example, suppose you want to see what happens to an ant with poor vision. Go to the statistics screen and find your candidate ant, one with a vision gene of 0001, 0010, or 0011. When you find your candidate, retrieve its ID number from the second column, and press Escape to return to the menu. Now press C, type your ant's ID number, and press Enter. Finally, press Escape to return to the menu, and press R to return to the simulation. Watch the white ant. Unless it's extremely lucky, it will soon die of starvation and disappear from the screen.

Conclusion

The a-life programs studied in research labs are often much more complex than those presented here, of course. Many are so complex, in fact, that they won't even run on desktop computers, and instead function only on some of the largest computers ever built. Still, regardless of a program's underlying complexity, the basic techniques remain the same.

Modest hardware requirements notwithstanding, the programs in this chapter are fascinating examples of a-life in action. Unfortunately, not all a-life programmers apply their often considerable talents to the advancement of their field. Instead, they create a-life programs with a sole purpose of wreaking havoc on computers the world over. In the next chapter, you'll learn about these pesky forms of a-life, commonly called *computer viruses*.

Appetite for Destruction: Computer Viruses

What do the following pieces of software have in common?

Stoned
4096
Cascade
Jerusalem
Michelangelo
Cookie Monster
Tequila
Joshi
Pakistani Brain
Crabs

No, they're not the latest best-selling games. They're computer viruses, insidious a-life programs that replicate in a computer, passing from system to system like a digital flu. Sadly, although you might not know

it, one of these viruses (or any one of thousands of others) may have already infected your system. If this thought makes you nervous, you're not alone. Every day, millions of computer owners expend valuable time and effort—not to mention hundreds of dollars—ensuring that their systems stay free of these computerized diseases.

What exactly are computer viruses? Where did they come from? How can you tell if your system is infected, and what can you do if it is? Can you avoid infection altogether? In this chapter, you learn the answers to these questions. In addition, you have a chance to see viruses in action, when you run the virus simulations included on your book disk.

What Is a Computer Virus?

A computer virus isn't actually a disease; it's a small a-life program capable of replicating itself in a computer and spreading to other systems, usually through floppy disks or programs downloaded from a BBS (see Figure 4.1). You can minimize your chances of introducing one of these dastardly programs into your computer system, but if your computer is infected, a virus can attach itself to many programs and disks before you're aware of its presence, making the infection difficult to stamp out.

It's important to remember that a computer virus is simply a program, and like any other program you have on your system, a virus can't do anything until you run it. Unfortunately, viruses have many clever ways of ensuring that you run them. For example, you might download what seems to be a great game from a local BBS. When you run the game, it seems to perform as advertised—but along with your alien blasting or dungeon exploring, the program infects your system with a computer virus. The worst part is that you will have no idea—at least, not until it's too late—that anything untoward is happening.

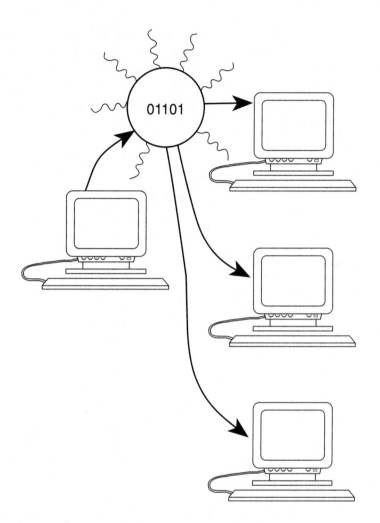

Figure 4.1.

Computer viruses are small programs that replicate and spread from system to system.

Where do computer viruses come from? Computer programmers create them, of course. Talented programmers waste their skills on such troublesome ventures for a broad range of reasons. Maybe the programmer just wants to create the ultimate computer practical joke, in which case the virus might do little more than flash a brief message on-screen. A programmer with a malicious nature or a grudge, however, might want to cause as much destruction as possible. This person's virus can do anything from corrupt data files to physically damage the computer. Then, of course, there is the stereotypical hacker who prefers the company of his or her computer to that of other humans (see Figure 4.2). Although not all antisocial hackers turn their talents toward destruction, there are those who do.

Figure 4.2.

Some computer hackers much prefer the company of their computers to the company of other human beings.

Viruses are becoming more and more dangerous these days because of increased communication among computers (Figure 4.3). Most computers today participate in some sort of network activity. Whether a computer is part of a small office network or connected to millions of other computers through commercial networks like CompuServe, Delphi, or GEnie, a network offers the computer virus a perfect channel through which to propagate. Privately owned BBSs, which are the most likely places for downloading an infected program (you have no way of knowing what kind of person the owner is), are springing up in greater numbers than ever before. With so many computers in contact with each other, the potential for widespread data destruction is mind boggling.

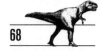

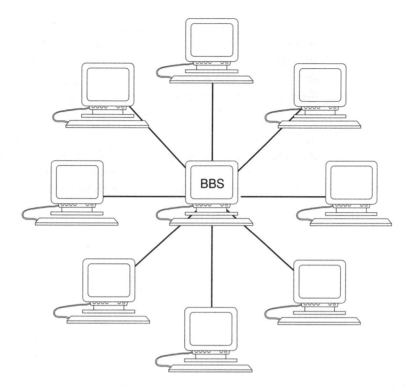

Figure 4.3.

Because of increased connectivity among computers, viruses are more dangerous than ever.

Types of Computer Viruses

You can sort the thousands of different computer viruses into four basic categories: innocuous, comical, data-altering, and catastrophic (see Figure 4.4).

- *Innocuous viruses* replicate and spread just like other viruses, but they have no effect (at least, no deliberate effect) on the systems they infect. Instead, they simply install themselves on the system and sit dormant. Programmers create this kind of virus simply for the thrill of seeing their programs propagate around the world.

- *Comical viruses,* on the other hand, might display messages on-screen, alter the screen display, or perform some other type of joke. This type of virus can be annoying, but causes no intentional damage.

● *Data-altering viruses,* on the other hand, change data on a hard drive, introducing errors into spreadsheets, databases, and other similar data-intensive applications. Because data-altering viruses often do their work over a long period of time, their effects are subtle; but, as you can imagine, errors introduced into critical data often lead to disastrous results.

● Finally, *catastrophic viruses,* the worst of the lot, typically erase critical files or even destroy all data on a hard drive. People have even reported finding viruses that cause actual physical damage to a computer system, although these are extremely rare.

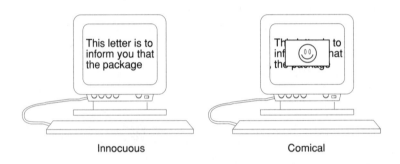

Innocuous   Comical

Figure 4.4.

Viruses can be grouped into four types: innocuous, comical, data-altering, and catastrophic.

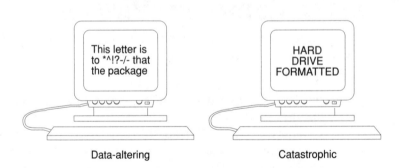

Data-altering   Catastrophic

Whose crazy idea was it to create these annoying, often malicious, forms of a-life? You might be surprised to learn that, at first, it was simply a few respectable computer scientists having a little fun among themselves.

An Excerpt From...

The History of Computer Viruses

Programmers at the AT&T Bell Laboratories and Xerox Corporation's research center developed the first viruses in the 1970s, playing what they called "Core Wars." Participants created computer "organisms" designed to destroy an opponent's similar creations.

These computer organisms were capable of self-replication, but incapable of spreading to other systems; they were destroyed when the user turned off the machine. Moreover, in the 70s, the sophisticated networks of today were not in place, so a virus had no place to go. Nevertheless, these simple viruses soon displayed their unpredictable nature when one strain went out of control on a Xerox 530, forcing management to call a halt to the programmer's games.

Luckily, the programmers who created these early computer viruses were responsible, knowledgeable professionals who knew that the techniques with which they had been experimenting could be dangerous in the wrong hands. As a result, these early experimenters kept secret most of what they learned about self-replicating programs.

In 1984, the creation of computer viruses became public knowledge. *Scientific American* magazine published an article describing computer viruses, including an offer that allowed readers to obtain, for two dollars, instructions on how to program viruses. Although this article opened the proverbial Pandora's box, viruses that appeared over the next couple of years were practical jokes (mostly created on college campuses) and rarely appeared on personal computers. These jokes turned sour, however, as more powerful and destructive viruses made themselves known.

By 1986, hobbyist programmers had attained the skills needed to create computer viruses on personal computers. Computer networks and BBSs were also becoming increasingly popular, so the creators of this new generation of viruses had convenient channels through which to quickly and easily release their creations on an unsuspecting public. By 1988, computer viruses were an epidemic (see Figure 4.5).

Epidemic notwithstanding, people still considered these tiny, self-replicating a-life programs minor pests. Then, in November of 1988, Robert Morris, Jr., a computer hacker at Cornell University, created what he thought was an innocuous virus. He released the virus into the InterNet network, assuming it would invisibly attach one copy of itself to every connected system. But an error in programming caused the virus to reproduce uncontrollably. Before the dust settled, the virus brought the network, which included many important research facilities, to its knees. The virus infected over 6,000 systems on the InterNet, and the restoration process cost nearly $100 million dollars. Morris, although mortified by his mistake, had taught the world that even "safe" viruses could be nasty indeed.

How Viruses Work

Most computer viruses, regardless of their effect on a system, follow the same life cycle. This life cycle includes four phases (see Figure 4.6):

1. Introduction

2. Infection

3. Replication

4. Activation

In the *introduction phase,* the user unknowingly places a virus-infected disk into a floppy drive or installs a "Trojan Horse" program (a program that hides a computer virus) on her or his computer. At this point, the virus has not yet infiltrated the machine. To infiltrate the computer, the virus must be executed, which occurs in the infection phase.

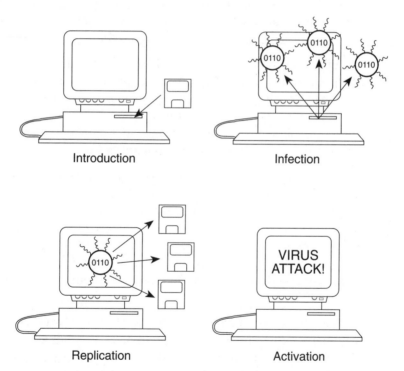

Introduction

Infection

Replication

Activation

Figure 4.6.

A computer virus's life cycle includes four phases.

The *infection phase* begins when the user boots his computer with the infected floppy disk in the drive, or when he runs the program carrying the virus. In both cases, the virus program executes. It quickly separates from its host (the infected disk or program) and searches for safe places in which to copy itself. These safe places include application programs, the boot sectors of other floppy disks

currently in the system's drives, or even the computer's operating system.

Once the virus has infiltrated the system, it enters its *replication phase*. At this point, the user doesn't know the system has been infected. The virus bides its time, infecting new floppy disks placed into the system's drives, attaching itself to newly installed program files, or even hitching a ride with files uploaded through the telephone lines.

The virus continues the replication phase until it reaches its *activation phase*, which can be a specific date (Friday the 13th is a popular virus-activation date), a count of virus replications, the passing of a specific period of time (a week, a month, or a year), or some other criteria the creator chose. The virus then sets about performing whatever mischief its creator designed it to do.

Unfortunately, even in this latter phase, the user might not suspect the presence of a virus. "Typos" might appear in a word-processor document, or an incorrect value in a spreadsheet—caused by the virus, but blamed on human error. The user fixes the errors and carries on, oblivious to the virus. Only after the virus strikes again and again might the user suspect something wrong.

Less subtle viruses, on the other hand, immediately make themselves known. They might intermittently change the screen display, erase files, or even reformat a hard disk. The user might still not suspect a computer virus infection, perhaps blaming the sudden disaster on hardware failure. Because a virus's effects on the system are often similar to hardware malfunctions, a user might assume the system needs repair and spend money for unnecessary work (Figure 4.7).

By now the infection has already run its course, regardless of whether the user discovers it during its activation phase. Many of the user's programs and floppy disks are infected, as well as any copies inadvertently passed to other users. This is why computer virus infections are so difficult to eradicate: the user can successfully rid the computer of the virus, only to insert an infected floppy disk into a drive at a later date and reintroduce the virus to the system. Dozens, or even hundreds, of the user's disks might be infected before the user discovers the virus.

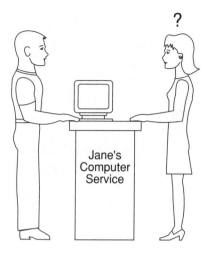

Jane's
Computer
Service

Figure 4.7.

Viruses often mimic hardware failures, causing users to bring their systems in for unnecessary repairs.

In addition, removing a virus from a computer system is often a difficult task. For example, a virus that controls the computer's operating system can intercept commands the user issues to the computer. If the user tries to remove the virus, the virus protects itself by not allowing the computer to respond to the command. Even worse, the virus might be clever enough to fool the user into thinking that it has been removed. In this case, the virus might allow the system to return to normal operation for a given period of time, then strike again.

To make a bad situation even worse, the current crop of *stealth* viruses is inordinately skillful at disguising its presence. Some of these treacherous programs cloak themselves by hiding behind the operating system, intercepting commands that might reveal their presence and producing results that look normal to the user who's searching for them. The 4096 (or Frodo) virus, which damages data on a hard drive, works this way.

Other stealth viruses use fancy encryption techniques to vary the virus's binary code, so that each copy of the virus in the system looks different. These encryption techniques make the virus virtually impossible to locate. The Tequila, Telecom, and Holocaust viruses all hide themselves through encryption techniques, and all eventually damage disk files.

Recognizing the Effects of Viruses

The effects of viruses are as diverse as the viruses themselves. Anything you can program a computer to do is fair game for a virus. Some viruses might simply display a humorous message. Others might work their way through a hard drive, changing random pieces of data as they go. Still others might suddenly fill the computer's memory with copies of themselves, causing the system to lock up. The worst viruses quickly and efficiently destroy all data on the system's drives, leaving the system completely useless until you can recover the data. (And, of course, unless you backed up the lost data, you might never restore it. Worse yet, restoring backed-up data might also restore the virus!)

How can you know whether a computer virus has infected your system? It's tough to answer that question. In most cases, suspected virus infections are traced to real system failures—a corrupted hard drive, for example, or maybe a flaky memory chip. The fact is, although computer viruses are as numerous as ants at a picnic, most system malfunctions are not symptoms of virus infections.

Luckily, some viruses are obvious and easy to spot the instant they reach their activation phase. For example, the Crabs virus, which first infected Macintosh computers, causes small insects to appear and begin eating the screen display. Talk about program bugs! Obviously, the Crabs virus is rarely confused with hardware problems. Likewise, the Sex virus, which first appeared on IBM compatibles and displays some rather...ahem...explicit graphics, is not likely to fool a savvy computer user for long.

Although some viruses are a snap to spot, others cause problems easily mistaken for hardware failures. The Lehigh and Michelangelo viruses, for example, destroy all data on the infected system's drives. But anyone who uses hard drives knows that, sooner or later, the drive will become unbootable; why should they immediately suspect a virus?

How To Avoid Viruses

You might not be able to avoid all computer viruses, but you can drastically reduce your chances of infection by following a few simple rules.

1. If you don't have a hard drive, always boot your system from the same floppy disk. Keep this disk write-protected. You must be sure, of course, that this boot disk is not already infected.

2. If you have a hard drive, avoid booting your system from a floppy. If, for some reason, you must boot from a floppy, follow the rules in step one.

3. Avoid placing disks from other computers into your machine. If you have to share files with someone, transfer the files over a network, to reduce (not eliminate) the chance of virus infection.

4. Download programs only from reputable BBSs or commercial online services. All downloaded software should be treated with suspicion, but if you run a program you obtained from a pirate BBS, you significantly increase your chances of a virus infection.

5. If you want to use shareware, test the software from its own directory. Never run shareware from your drive's root directory.

6. Do not run pirated software. Use commercial products purchased at a reputable store and still in their shrink-wrapped package. Pirated versions of commercial software are infamous for carrying viruses.

NOTE: No matter how hard you try, no matter how well you follow the antivirus rules, your computer can still come down with a virus infection. Luckily, you can purchase several top-notch virus detection and removal programs—including Norton AntiVirus and Central Point Anti-Virus—at your nearest software store. Although these programs cannot guarantee a 100 percent success rate, they can detect and remove thousands of known viruses. More important, they are continually updated to handle new viruses that appear. If you buy an antivirus program, use it regularly.

Your Own Virus Demonstration

All this talk about viruses can't replace actually experiencing one. On the disk provided with this book you'll find five programs that demonstrate the effects of the Cascade, Denzuk, Italian, Jerusalem, and Music viruses. To install these programs, please refer to the last page of the book, facing the disk.

> **NOTE:** Remember that these programs on the disk are not real viruses; they're only virus simulations. You cannot hurt your computer by running them.

The Cascade Virus

The first simulation in the set is the Cascade virus, which has the file name CASC-SIM.COM. To run the program, change to the \ALIFE\VIRUS directory, type **CASC-SIM**, and press Enter. After the program installs itself as a *terminate-and-stay-resident* (TSR) program, a message appears on-screen telling you the virus is ready to go. Run your favorite DOS application and sit back for the fun.

Cascade, like all the simulations in the set, is an example of a comical virus. In this case, the virus makes letters fall down the screen. Much like a goofy game of Tetris, the letters fall until they hit an obstruction, where they slowly pile up as the virus becomes more and more active. The longer you run the virus, the faster the letters fall. Figure 4.8 shows the DOS editor's screen after an attack of the Cascade virus.

When you've seen enough of Cascade, remove it from memory by pressing Alt-Minus (Alt plus the minus key on the numeric keypad).

The Denzuk Virus

The Denzuk virus, a simulation on your disk with the file name DENZ-SIM.COM, is a bit more subtle than the Cascade virus. This fellow sits in memory waiting for the user to hit the Ctrl-Alt-Delete keystroke, at which point the virus flashes its colorful and tastefully drawn signature, as shown in Figure 4.9.

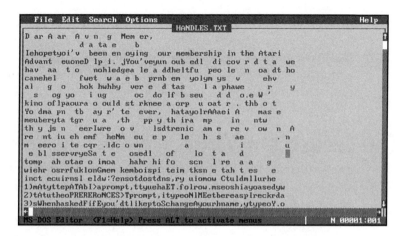

```
 File  Edit  Search  Options                                    Help
                              HANDLES.TXT
 D  ar A  ar  A  v  n  g  Mem er,
         d  a t a e    b
 Iehopetyoi'v  been en oying  our membership in the Atari
 Advant  euoneD  lp i. jYou' veyun oub edl  di cov r d t a  we
 hav  aa  t o   nohledgea le a ddheltfu  peo le  n  oa dt ho
 canehel    fwet  w a e b  prnb em  yolym ys  v    ehv
 al   g  o  hok hwhhy  ver e  d tas      l a phawe    r    y
    s    og yo  i ug      oc  do lf b seu   d d  o.e W '
 kino oflpaoura o ould st rknee a orp  u oat r . thb o t
 Yo dma pn  tb  ay r' te  ever,  hatayolrAAaei A    mas e
 meuberyta tgr  u a ,th   pp y th ira  mp    in   ntw
 th y js n   eerIwre  o v   lsdtrenic  am e  re v  ow  n A
 re  nt iu eh emf  heNm  eu  e  p  le   h  s   ae      . n
 m eero i te cqr .ldc o wn        a          i         u
  e bl sservryeSa t e   osedl  of   lo t a  d
 tomp  ah otae o imoa   hahr hi fo   scn  l re  a a   g
 wiehr osrrfuklonGmen kemboispi tein tksn e tah t es  e
 inct ecuirnsl eldw:?ensotdostdns,ry uiomow Ctuldmllurhe
 1)mAtyttepATAbI>aprompt,ttyuehaET.folrow.mseoshiayoasedyw
 2)tAtutheoPRERERoNCES>Yprompt,itypeoNlMEetbereaspIreckrda
 3)sWhenhaskedFifEyou'dtlikeptoSchangeAyourhname,ytypeoY.o
 MS-DOS Editor  <F1=Help> Press ALT to activate menus        N 00001:001
```

Figure 4.8.

The Cascade virus doing its thing.

To run the Denzuk simulation, change to the \ALIFE\VIRUS directory, type **DENZ-SIM**, and press Enter. You see the screen shown in Figure 4.10. Press any key to see Denzuk's display. Because the Denzuk simulation is not a TSR, you don't have to remove it from memory after running it.

Figure 4.9.

The Denzuk virus in action.

```
 British Computer Virus Research Centre      (Tel: 0273-26105)
 12 Guildford Street, Brighton, East Sussex, BN1 3LS, England

 Virus Simulation Suite                   Written by Joe Hirst

       Program                DENZ-SIM.COM V1.10
       Denzuk virus - single shot display

            Copyright (c) Joe Hirst 1989, 1990.

       This program is NOT a virus, nor is it infectious

       Press any key when ready to observe display
```

Figure 4.10.

The Denzuk virus simulation's starting screen.

The Italian Virus

One of your author's favorites, the Italian virus, is next on the list. This amusing virus bounces a white ball across the user's screen. To run the Italian virus simulation, change to the \ALIFE\VIRUS directory, type **ITL-SIMX**, and press Enter. You can start the program also by adding a parameter representing the number of minutes for the virus to wait before the ball appears. For example, to have the ball appear after one minute, run the program by typing **ITL-SIMX 1**. If you run the program without the parameter, the ball appears immediately. To remove the TSR program from memory, press Alt-Minus.

The Jerusalem Virus

The Jerusalem virus is a little different from the other viruses you've seen because you can mistake its effects for real hardware or software problems. When activated, this virus shifts a portion of the screen up two rows, leaving a blank space on the display. As you can see from Figure 4.11, the effects are alarming.

To run the Jerusalem virus simulation, change to the \ALIFE\VIRUS directory, type **JERU-SIM**, and press Enter. You can also start Jerusalem by adding a parameter representing the number of minutes for the virus to wait before striking. If you run the program without the parameter, the delay is automatically one minute. To remove the Jerusalem TSR from memory, press Alt-Minus.

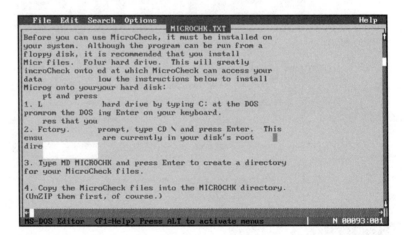

Figure 4.11.

The effects of the Jerusalem virus.

The Music Virus

The last demonstration, the Music virus, plays various tunes at preset intervals. Imagine you're hard at work on a spreadsheet when your computer suddenly breaks into a rousing version of "Stars and Stripes Forever"!

To run the Music virus simulation, change to the \ALIFE\VIRUS directory, type **ORO-SIMX**, and press Enter. The first tune plays almost immediately, with other tunes starting at half-minute intervals. To remove the Music TSR from memory, press Alt-Minus.

Conclusion

Although computer viruses are a fascinating example of a-life (due mostly to their capability to reproduce), they can be immensely destructive. With a little care, you can protect your system from infection. But as the InterNet fiasco demonstrated, people cannot ignore a virus's potential for creating worldwide havoc. Imagine, for example, a future in which terrorists employ computer viruses in attacking political or corporate enemies. When you consider that every major government in the world relies heavily on computers, you can't help but shudder. Computer viruses are, in fact, this planet's first run-in with a fearsome artificial life form that has the power to cause widespread destruction. Frightening, no?

The Silicon Brain: Artificial Intelligence

As you've learned, artificial intelligence (AI) plays a critical role in the development of artificial life. Programmers use AI techniques to control a-life simulations, and sometimes even to create computer programs that mimic human intelligence. But what exactly is AI?

The truth is, there is no set-in-stone definition for this important field of study. Although most researchers agree that the goal of AI studies is to make machines smarter and to study the nature of intelligence, few can agree on a general definition. Some even say that because there is no standard definition, AI is not actually a science, but rather simply a software-engineering discipline.

An Excerpt From...

Alan Bundy's "What Kind of Field Is AI?"

AI may be difficult to define because there are several types of AI. In his paper "What Kind of Field Is AI?," Alan Bundy breaks AI study into three fields (see Figure 5.1 also):

1. *Applied AI:* Commercial and industrial uses of AI fall into this category. For example, AI used to control an assembly robot is applied AI, as is an expert system designed to help doctors more quickly diagnose illness.

2. *Cognitive science:* In this branch of AI, researchers use AI techniques to try to better understand the workings of natural intelligence.

3. *Basic AI:* Here, researchers look for better ways to simulate intelligence on a computer.

Although these three types of AI have clearly defined goals, it's hard to draw a line between them. For example, studies in basic AI lead to computer algorithms that programmers use in applied or cognitive AI; and the results of studies in cognitive science provide ample clues for new directions of research in basic AI.

Patrick Henry Winston, a professor of computer science at MIT and the author of the textbook *Artificial Intelligence,* defines AI as "the study of the computations that make it possible to perceive, reason, and act." This definition partly describes both applied AI and cognitive science, the first two branches of AI study listed previously; but it precisely defines only basic AI.

The waters grow murkier when you consider whether you can actually define a machine as intelligent. Because one usually associates intelligence with living things, one returns to the controversy over whether artificial life is actually alive. Can a machine truly be intelligent? To answer this question, you first need a definition of intelligence.

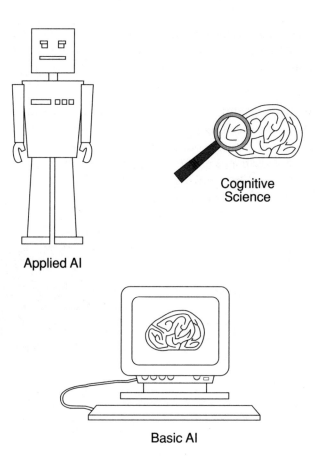

Cognitive
Science

Applied AI

Basic AI

Figure 5.1.

*There are three
fields of artificial
intelligence
research.*

What Is Intelligence?

Webster's New World Dictionary defines intelligence as "the ability to
learn or understand from experience; ability to acquire and retain
knowledge." You've already discovered that computer neural
networks learn from experience. They also acquire and retain
knowledge. After all, a neural network that can't retain what it
learned is useless. Expert systems, another common form of AI, also
learn, acquire, and retain knowledge. Does this prove that machines
are intelligent?

Maybe there is a more scientific definition of intelligence. How
about defining intelligence as "the manipulation of meaningless

abstract symbols such that these symbols take on meanings relative to objects and states-of-being in the real world." (I based this definition on George Lakoff's definition of human reason in his book *Women, Fire, and Dangerous Things.*)

Imagine reading a book. The words in the book are abstract symbols that have meaning to you only when you can associate the words to the world around you. The word *tree,* for example, is just some lines scribbled on a page, but when you relate the symbol *tree* to that tall and leafy thing growing in your front yard, you've demonstrated intelligence. (See Figure 5.2.)

Figure 5.2.

The word tree is a meaningless symbol until you use intelligence to relate the symbol to an actual tree.

Can a computer demonstrate this form of intelligence? To continue with the tree example, an optical character recognition system can read the word tree from a page. After the word is in the computer's memory, even a 10-year-old programmer can write a simple instruction such as, "If word equals tree, draw a tree." In this case, the computer reads the word tree and associates it with the real object (or, at least, a picture of the real object). So machines can be intelligent after all!

If you find this logic a little weak, you're not alone. Many leading researchers object vehemently to these assumptions—assumptions that others in the AI field make about the human mind. These researchers claim that we are far from understanding even the simplest details of how the human mind works, and it's absurd to assume that computers can be intelligent in the same way humans are.

So, although a general definition for AI may not be easy to formulate, maybe we can list some characteristics important to AI. Roger C. Schank, in his article "What Is AI Anyway?," lists nine important characteristics of AI systems:

- *Representation.* Represents knowledge in a useful and easily interpretable way.

- *Decoding.* Takes input from the real world and translates it into an internal representation.

- *Inference.* Applies meaning to input. In other words, an AI system should be capable of extracting meaning from a limited knowledge base.

- *Control of Combinational Explosion.* Recognizes when it knows enough about a particular subject and when it is going down false paths.

- *Indexing.* Has an efficient way of extracting data from its knowledge base.

- *Prediction and recovery.* Predicts events within its area of knowledge and can analyze and explain faulty predictions.

- *Dynamic modification.* Is capable of learning.

- *Generalization.* Is able to apply experience in order to devise more general solutions.

- *Curiosity.* The ultimate AI system will be capable of creative processes. Curiosity will impel the system to explore original methods for handling problems.

Why Does It Matter?

When it comes to practical considerations, researchers in AI don't much care what their critics say. They're only interested in making machines smarter, which they've done. To those who work in applied and basic AI, whether their computer programs mimic the way the brain actually works is irrelevant. The fact is, their systems display intelligence, an intelligence that can make solving certain types of computing problems easier.

If studying the human mind leads to new ways to write intelligent programs, so much the better. Neural networks, for example, are modeled after what scientists have learned about the structure of the human brain. The implementation of a neural network on a computer may or may not actually resemble the way the brain learns, but it does work on a computer. And as long as an AI technique works, who cares whether it actually mimics the human brain?

AI versus the Brain

How difficult is it to duplicate the actual abilities of the human brain, anyway? Consider this question in terms of a neural network. Today's most powerful computers can handle about 100 million neural connections. That sounds like a bunch until you realize that even a lowly insect boasts over one billion neural connections (see Figure 5.3).

Figure 5.3.

Even a lowly insect boasts over one billion neural connections.

Obviously, a human's intellectual capacity goes a bit beyond an insect's. In fact, scientists believe that the human brain comprises 10^{11} neurons (100,000,000,000, or 100 billion), each of which may be connected to as many as 100,000 other neurons. On average, then, there are 10^{16} (10,000,000,000,000,000 or 10 quadrillion) connections in the human brain. Obviously, without some miraculous advances in computer science, it'll be a good long time, if ever, before we can mimic the full power of the human brain electronically.

Luckily, most AI applications need not be as flexible, or deal with as many situations, as the human brain. For example, a computer program designed to play chess need be concerned only with intelligently applying the rules and strategies of chess. If you've ever played chess against a computer, you know how smart these programs are.

In the long run, we might not be able to create computer programs that think as effectively as humans do. But in their own machine-like way, computer programs *do* think.

Symbolic and Non-Symbolic Intelligence

One result of the definition debate is different ways of viewing AI. Specifically, one can divide AI techniques into symbolic and non-symbolic approaches. The symbolic view—often represented by rule-based systems that manipulate discrete symbols to determine a result—sticks to the traditional paradigms developed early in AI research. The symbolic view works well when you apply it to problems you can reduce to a set of questions with yes/no answers. However, symbolic AI shows its weaknesses when you present it with situations that aren't so black and white.

Expert systems, which you'll read about later in this chapter, are an example of the symbolic approach to AI. These types of systems often derive an answer to a problem by asking a series of yes/no questions. By way of illustration, suppose someone is trying to use an expert system to identify a tree. The expert system asks questions such as "Is it a plant?" and "Does it have bark?," to which the person must answer yes or no. The questions continue until the expert system determines the name of the object.

The non-symbolic view is represented by *neural networks*. This approach to AI considers intelligence not as a symbol-processing mechanism, but as a vast collection of nodes that, by placing more emphasis on certain connections, can manipulate inputs so the results fall somewhere between yes and no. Think of that tree again. Although every tree looks like a tree, no two trees look exactly alike. Still, your mind is capable of identifying a tree (see Figure 5.4).

Figure 5.4.

The human mind is capable of recognizing a tree, regardless of the type of tree it is.

You can use the same *fuzzy logic* in computers to develop a system for character recognition. The letter *A* in Times Roman type looks different from the letter *A* in Courier type, yet they are both the same letter. By feeding many examples of the letter *A* into a neural network, evaluating the output, and modifying the strength of the connections so future output is closer to accurate, the network can learn to recognize the letter *A* in many different type styles. The output of such a network is never yes or no, however; it's a value that represents the likelihood of the result, a value somewhere between 0 (no) and 1 (yes). What the heck is *fuzzy logic,* anyway? Read on to find out.

Hybrid AI Systems

Because of its capability to handle uncertain input, a neural network is clearly better suited to creating a knowledge base from real-world input. However, once you have created that knowledge base, a symbolic system is often more adept at handling it. This complementary relationship indicates that perhaps the best solution is some sort of hybrid system that combines the best of both approaches to AI.

To make programs smarter, scientists are now combining various AI techniques to create hybrid systems. For example, by combining a neural network with an expert system, a computer program can create a knowledge base from real-world, fuzzy input. After the program creates that knowledge base, the program can use the simpler, rule-based system to access information quickly and easily.

Another hybrid system uses an expert system to train a neural network. The operator feeds the data in the expert system into the network, and the network evaluates its output by matching its results to that of the expert system. Yet another hybrid system uses an expert system to direct input to one of several neural networks by determining which network is best suited to handle the data.

The point is that each approach to AI programming has its strengths and weaknesses. There's no reason to favor one over another. To do so would be to throw the good away with the bad.

Expert Systems

If you were to flip through an AI textbook, you'd likely be overwhelmed by the discussions you saw there. Luckily, you already know about neural networks and genetic algorithms, both of which are used in AI research, so I won't discuss these topics further. You've been reading a lot about expert systems, too, but you've learned little about the way they work.

Fuzzy Logic

Fuzzy logic is a way for computers to deal with the many ambiguities present in the world. Different types of trees and letters in different fonts are just two examples of the huge amount of "fuzzy" data with which the human mind must deal. When a computer can handle these types of uncertainties, it becomes more prepared to assist people with real-world problems.

Traditionally, computer logic deals with true or false conditions, which are represented by the values 1 and 0, respectively. By using fuzzy logic, however, a computer makes decisions that lie somewhere between these two absolutes.

In a way, fuzzy logic allows computers to use judgment in their processes. A new type of air conditioner created by Mitsubishi, for example, uses fuzzy logic to keep air temperature more consistent. Rather than turning on and off at preset levels, Mitsubishi's air conditioner is controlled by logic that says, in effect "When the room is too chilly, power down a little. When the room is too warm, power up a little." In order to use this type of logic, the air conditioner's computer controller must use judgment to decide what qualifies as too chilly and too warm.

Fuzzy logic has been used also to control the speed of subways more smoothly, to judge the dirtiness of clothes in a washing machine, and to adjust a vacuum cleaner to the amount of dust it must pick up. Fuzzy logic is even being used to help make stock-market decisions and to take better pictures with video cameras. The use of fuzzy logic is yet another way computers are beginning to think more like humans.

An expert system is simply a computer program that takes the place of a knowledgeable human being. Although an expert system cannot fully replace a thinking human, there are reasons to prefer an expert system to a human being. For example, if you were running your own company and had many employees to train, you might want to rely on an expert system to handle much of the training, because a computer does not require a paycheck, does not go hunting for a new job, and does not age and retire. Once you have your expert system running, it is often a more dependable source of information than any human being might be.

There are all types of expert systems, each with its own method of representing and accessing knowledge. The *rule-based* expert system is probably the easiest to understand, as it relies only on true or false conditions to formulate its output. Rule-based systems can demonstrate surprisingly realistic intelligence simply by translating the answers to a series of yes/no questions into the desired result. Programmers use rule-based expert systems in everything from simple programs that categorize objects to sophisticated systems that diagnose diseases.

Simple expert systems follow a structure called a *rule-based decision tree* to arrive at their output. Figure 5.5 shows the decision tree that might be used to identify a tree. In this case, the program starts by asking "Is it an animal?" The answer to this question is, of course, no, so the program follows the "no" branch of the tree to the question "Is it a mineral?" Again, the answer is no. The program follows the no branch to the question "Does it have bark?" This time the answer is yes, which brings the program to the answer of "tree."

Figure 5.5 is, of course, an oversimplification. A real expert system contains hundreds, even thousands, of questions, each bringing the user closer to the desired answer. After you build a complete expert system, it can be surprisingly astute in its evaluation of problems. So astute, in fact, that expert systems can plan a trip, train a new employee, and even help a doctor quickly diagnose a disease. In fact, in Chapter 8, "A-Life Off the Shelf—Commercial A-life Programs," you learn about a program called "The Home Medical Advisor," which you can use on your home computer. This program uses an expert system to help you diagnose medical problems at home.

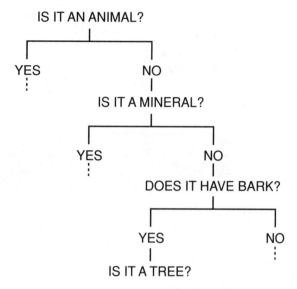

IS IT AN ANIMAL?

YES

NO

IS IT A MINERAL?

YES

NO

DOES IT HAVE BARK?

YES

NO

IS IT A TREE?

Figure 5.5.

Some expert systems use a decision tree to determine an answer to a problem.

But does an expert system represent artificial life? Well, not the same way a computer virus does. After all, expert systems don't replicate. However, a good expert system makes a computer a handy consultant, not unlike a human expert who answers questions about a particular procedure or subject. Moreover, you can update expert systems easily with new information. When the system fails to come up with a correct answer, you can add a new question, or *rule,* to the program's knowledge base to ensure that the system can answer the inquiry next time around. In this basic way, an expert system asks for and learns new information.

Guess the Animal: A Game That Learns

Two sample expert systems are on your book disk. The first, a game called Guess the Animal, enables you to build your own expert system by adding questions to an already existing knowledge base. (To install the program on your computer, please refer to the last page of this book, facing the disk.)

To run Guess the Animal, change to the \ALIFE\ANIMAL directory, type **ANIMAL**, and press Enter. (You must have the file
ANIMAL.DAT in the same directory as the program file.) When you
see the shareware screen, press Enter again to receive the program's
title screen, as shown in Figure 5.6. The game's instructions are on
this screen.

```
─ A R T I F I C I A L   I N T E L L I G E N C E ─
> > >   G U E S S   T H E   A N I M A L   < < <
                Version 3.01


You think of an animal...
                              ...and I will try to guess what it is.

If I guess incorrectly, you can tell me what animal you were thinking of,
then type in a `question' that would distinguish my animal from yours...

THE MORE I PLAY, THE SMARTER I GET!


                                          Hit any key when ready...
```

Figure 5.6.

*Guess the
Animal's title
screen.*

The program asks questions about an animal of which you're
thinking. If the program guesses the animal, the game ends. If the
program can't guess the animal, it asks for a new question, one
that distinguishes the animal you're thinking of from the one the
computer guessed. After you enter this question, the program will
have learned a new animal. By adding new animals to the program
in this way, you slowly build a powerful expert system that can
determine almost any animal possible.

Play a couple of games to see how the program works. Suppose
you're thinking of a dog. To start the game from the title screen,
press any key. You are asked

`Are you thinking of an Animal? (Y)es or (N)o...?`

Press Y to play the game or press N to go to Guess the Animal's
main menu. For now, press Y, followed by Enter. The program asks

`DOES IT HAVE FOUR LEGS?`

Because a dog has four legs, press Y, followed by Enter. The program then asks

IS IT A RODENT?

A dog is not a rodent, so answer N. The program asks

IS IT AN AMPHIBIAN?

A dog is not an amphibian, so answer N. The program then asks

IS IT A REPTILE?

A dog is not a reptile, so answer N. The program asks

Is it a DOG?

Answer Y. The program has successfully determined that you were thinking of a dog. Figure 5.7 shows the results of this first game.

```
Are you thinking of an animal?  (Y)es or (N)o...? y

DOES IT HAVE FOUR LEGS? y
IS IT A RODENT? n
IS IT AN AMPHIBIAN? n
IS IT A REPTILE? n
Is it a DOG? y

 Y E A H !  -  I knew that!...

Do you want to try another?
```

Figure 5.7.

Guess the Animal determines that you were thinking of a dog.

When the program asks Do you want to try another? answer Y. This time, suppose you're thinking of a house cat. Follow the preceding steps, but when the program asks whether the animal is a dog, press N. The program then prints the prompt

The animal you were thinking was a:

Type **HOUSE CAT** and then press Enter. The program requests

Please type in a QUESTION that would distinguish a HOUSE CAT from a DOG...

Type **IS IT A FELINE** and press Enter. (Note that you should not type a question mark.) The program asks

For a HOUSE CAT, the answer would be: ?

Answer Y. The program adds your question and answer to its knowledge base, and the game starts over. Figure 5.8 shows the house cat example as it appears on-screen.

```
Are you thinking of an animal?  (Y)es or (N)o...? y

DOES IT HAVE FOUR LEGS? y
IS IT A RODENT? n
IS IT AN AMPHIBIAN? n
IS IT A REPTILE? n
Is it a DOG? n
The animal you were thinking of was a: HOUSE CAT

Please type in a QUESTION that would distinguish
a HOUSE CAT from a DOG...
? IS IT A FELINE
For a HOUSE CAT, the answer would be: ? y
```

Figure 5.8.

Adding a house cat to the knowledge base.

After you enter the data for a house cat, play the game again to see how well the program does with the animal HOUSE CAT. As you can see by Figure 5.9, the program has learned something new.

```
Are you thinking of an animal?  (Y)es or (N)o...? y

DOES IT HAVE FOUR LEGS? y
IS IT A RODENT? n
IS IT AN AMPHIBIAN? n
IS IT A REPTILE? n
IS IT A FELINE? y
Is it a HOUSE CAT? y

 Y E A H !  -  I knew that!...

Do you want to try another?
```

Figure 5.9.

Guess the Animal has learned about house cats.

You can now add different types of felines, if you like, or maybe try a different type of animal entirely. (Figure 5.10 shows how the game might go if you were thinking of a lion.) Little by little, the program's animal knowledge base becomes larger and larger.

```
Are you thinking of an animal?  (Y)es or (N)o...? y

DOES IT HAVE FOUR LEGS? y
IS IT A RODENT? n
IS IT AN AMPHIBIAN? n
IS IT A REPTILE? n
IS IT A FELINE? y
Is it a HOUSE CAT? n
The animal you were thinking of was a: LION

Please type in a QUESTION that would distinguish
a LION from a HOUSE CAT...
? DOES IT LIVE IN AFRICA
For a LION, the answer would be: ? Y
```

Figure 5.10.

Now that Guess the Animal knows about felines, adding a new question allows it to distinguish between a house cat and a lion.

To return to the program's main menu, answer N when asked whether you want to try another animal. From the main menu, shown in Figure 5.11, choice 1 saves the current knowledge base to disk without exiting the program. Choice 2 erases everything you added to the knowledge base in the current session. Choice 3 lists all the animals in the current knowledge base. Choice 4 saves the current knowledge base and exits the program. And finally, choice 5 exits the program without saving the knowledge base.

```
                - E X I T   M E N U -


     1 - REMEMBER what I just learned

     2 - FORGET this session; start over

     3 - LIST what I know so far

     4 - SAVE this session, then Quit

     Q - QUIT without learning


   Esc - Go back...
```

Figure 5.11.

Guess the Animal's main menu.

A More Useful Expert System

Guess the Animal demonstrates how a simple expert system works. However, nothing beats having the real thing at your fingertips.

Although you can find several examples of useful expert systems on your local software store's shelves (you'll read about these programs in Chapter 8, "A-Life Off the Shelf—Commercial A-life Programs"), an expert system for fishermen, called (appropriately enough) Fish Expert System, is included on your book disk. By using this expert system, you can receive expert advice for your next fishing trip. (As usual, consult the last page of this book for installation instructions.)

To run Fish Expert System, change to the \ALIFE\FISHING directory, type **FISH**, and press Enter. You see the menu shown in Figure 5.12. To choose a menu item, press the appropriate number.

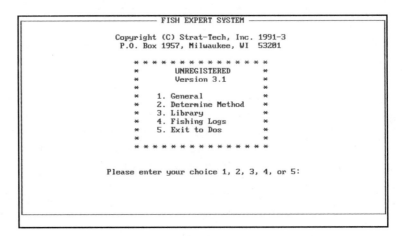

Figure 5.12.

Fish Expert System's main menu.

Press 1 (General) to access the overview screen, which provides you quick instructions for the menu and enables you to adjust the colors of the display. If you access this screen but do not want to change the display's colors, press E to return to the main menu.

Selection 2 (Determine Method) accesses the actual expert system. When you select this menu item, you see the main screen. Here, the program asks a series of questions for which you must supply yes/no answers, using 1 for yes and 2 for no. (Be forewarned: If you accidentally type Y or N instead of the required 1 or 2, the program displays an error message and returns you to the beginning. This design flaw can be frustrating if you make a mistake after having already answered several questions.)

After you answer the questions, Fish Expert System suggests a method for catching trout under the conditions you entered into the program, as shown in Figure 5.13. (This version of Fish Expert System is good only for trout fishing. The full version of the program is available for a fee from the authors.) Press Escape to return to the main menu.

```
┌──────────────── FISH EXPERT SYSTEM ────────────────┐
│ *When you answer yes to one value, answer no to the others.  For example, │
│  yes to morning requires no to midday; yes to spring, no to summer, autumn. │
│  To return to the main menu press 'Esc' twice.  To print or log results │
│  press 'Alt-P' and press return to toggle 'Printer' or 'Log file' on/off. │
│                                                    │
│  BELOW ENTER '1' FOR YES AND '2' FOR NO  (turn Num Lck on if desired) │
│                                                    │
│  Question:- after trout ? yes                      │
│  Question:- spring ? yes                           │
│  Question:- morning ? no                           │
│  Question:- mid day ? no                           │
│  Question:- afternoon ? yes                        │
│  Question:- lake ? yes                             │
│  Question:- medium winds ? no                      │
│  Question:- high winds ? no                        │
│  Question:- warm water temperature ? yes           │
│                                                    │
│  The best method is fly or spin cast with lures, bait at spring holes where │
│  cooler water temperatures attract trout - also troll springs - when you │
│  catch a trout, mark spot and troll over it again. │
│                                                    │
│  Press any key to continue                         │
└────────────────────────────────────────────────────┘
```

Figure 5.13.

The Fish Expert System main screen.

Selection 3 (Library) accesses Fish Expert System's information screen, where you can call up and read various information files on different aspects of fishing. (If you get a Path not found error, you need to use main menu item 1 to set the path to the data files.) Use your arrow keys to highlight the text file you want to read, and then press Enter. The program displays the file in a window, as shown in Figure 5.14. Use your arrow keys, or your PageUp and PageDown keys, to scroll through the file as you read. After reading the selected file, press Escape to return to the file selection screen, then press Escape a second time to return to the main menu.

Selection 4 (Fishing Logs) enables you to create fishing trip logs, equipment lists, lake descriptions, boating plans, packing lists, trip expense reports, and other text files that make fishing trips safer and easier to organize. The forms included with the program require only that you fill in the details and save the finished file to disk.

To exit Fish Expert System, press selection 5 (Exit to DOS).

```
┌─────────────────────── FISH EXPERT SYSTEM ───────────────────────┐
│ FISH SAFELY !!                                    Line 1     Col 1 │
├───────────────────────────────────────────────────────────────────┤
│   RECOMMENDED METHODS OF FISHING AND DEFINITION:                  │
│                                                                   │
│   Still fishing - positioning yourself in an area and using live bait. │
│                                                                   │
│   Casting - positioning yourself in an area and casting artificial or │
│             live bait or a combination using spinning or regular reels. │
│             Sometimes Bass fisherman like to "flip cast" which we │
│             describe as a short, accurate cast into cover openings to │
│             entice fish in the cover or other structure.   You    │
│             could not get to this cover with a long cast.         │
│                                                                   │
│   Trolling - using a moving boat to cover an area with live bait, │
│              artificials, or a combination.  This includes variants │
│              such as drift fishing, slipping, back trolling, etc.. │
│              You may also use downriggers or other methods to get │
│              the bait to the depth you want.                      │
│                                                                   │
│   Fly Fishing - using fly fishing rod and reel equipment and associated │
│                 lightweight flies, lures or live bait.            │
├───────────────────────────────────────────────────────────────────┤
│ PgDn PgUp Arrows  F2:Goto  F3:Srch  F10:End  C:\WINWORD\ALIFE\DISK\FISH\METHODS. │
└───────────────────────────────────────────────────────────────────┘
```

Figure 5.14.

The Fish Expert System enables you to display many helpful information files.

Although Fish Expert System may not be useful to everyone, you can see by experimenting with it how handy an expert system can be. Programmers can write similar expert systems for just about any area of expertise, making expert advice quickly and easily available without having to have an actual human expert on hand.

Conclusion

Expert systems demonstrate how even simple AI techniques can transform a computer into a machine that thinks. By sorting through data and determining the solution to a problem, the computer shows basic intelligence. And, as you know, intelligence is one characteristic that is present, to some extent or another, in most life forms.

In the next chapter, you'll take a look at the fascinating world of *robotics,* an area of study that combines engineering with a-life techniques to create mobile beings that can see, talk, and even adapt to their environment.

Silicon and Steel: The Study of Robotics

As creatures living in a physical world, people tend to associate life with physical characteristics. For this reason, people find it difficult to think that cells in a computer might be alive—or might even represent life in any reasonable fashion. Robots, however, are tangible objects. Because they exist in the same universe and are bound by the same restraints that the universe places on people, humans can more easily relate to them. Probably no other form of artificial life has so thoroughly captured the human imagination throughout history as robots and other similar human-made creatures.

In this chapter, you'll examine the history of robots from their mythical roots to fantastic visions of the future. Along the way, you'll meet a couple of the more interesting researchers in the field whose brilliance and dedication have moved the science of robotics from the automobile assembly lines into people's homes and possibly into the farthest reaches of the universe.

SILICON AND STEEL: THE STUDY OF ROBOTICS

The Dream of Creation

According to the Bible, God fabricated the first human being from the dust of the Earth. Ever since that divine creation, humans have searched for the elusive secret of life. From apocryphal tales passed down through the middle ages to the success stories of today's engineers and computer scientists, history brims over with artificial creatures.

Consider the medieval alchemist Paracelsus, for example, who developed a bizarre formula that (he claimed) could create a living human being from horse manure, human blood, and other ingredients sealed in a jar for forty days (see Figure 6.1). His *homunculus*, as he called the resulting creature, was supposed to emerge from its sealed jar as a fully formed, albeit tiny, infant. Paracelsus stated that this human-made infant should then be "...educated with the greatest care and zeal, until it grows and begins to display intelligence."

Figure 6.1.

Paracelsus claimed he could create a human being from horse manure, human blood, and other ingredients sealed in a jar for forty days.

Sixteenth century Hebrew legends also tell of artificial beings, called *golems,* which rabbis created from clay and empowered with life through the name of God. Although their creators charged them with protecting the Jews from their persecutors, the golems often ran amok instead, forcing their creators to destroy them.

Perhaps one of the most famous artificial beings is the monster created by Mary Shelley's fictional Dr. Frankenstein, undoubtedly inspired by the legend of the golems. Dr. Frankenstein created this creature from corpses and brought it to life with electricity. But, as

102

is often the case when humans try to aspire to God-hood, Frankenstein's monster proved to be more a curse than a scientific breakthrough.

None of these fictional creatures qualifies as a robot. They weren't machines, after all, but rather beings brought to life through magical or pseudo-scientific means. But the idea of mechanical beings goes back almost as far as the aforementioned myths. In fact, one can trace the first image of a robot to drawings by the seventeenth-century artist Giovanni Battista Braccelli.

Still, the word *robot,* based on the Czech word *robota,* meaning labor, wasn't coined until 1921, in the play *R.U.R.* by Karel Capek. R.U.R., which stands for "Rossum's Universal Robots," tells of artificial humans designed to work as slaves. These creatures began with no capacity for human emotions, but when the robots are given emotions, they revolt against their oppressors and destroy the human race.

Fritz Lang's classic movie *Metropolis,* released in 1926, also featured a killer robot. In this case, the robot disguised itself as a woman named Maria and tried to provoke human workers into destroying their underground environment. When the workers discover Maria's ulterior motives, they burn her, revealing not a creature of flesh, but one of steel.

Considering the havoc caused by the robots in *R.U.R.* and *Metropolis,* and the nastiness attributed to golems, rejuvenated corpses, and other beings born of the human imagination, one is correct in assuming that people viewed artificial creatures with distaste, if not outright fear. All this changed in 1942 when Isaac Asimov (see Figure 6.2) began writing his series of robot stories. Asimov's robots were dedicated to serving humankind, thanks to Asimov's Three Laws of Robotics:

1. A robot cannot injure a human being, or through inaction, allow a human being to come to harm.

2. A robot must obey the orders given to it by human beings except when such orders conflict with the First Law.

3. A robot must protect its existence as long as such protection does not conflict with the First or Second Law.

However, even Asimov (who is credited also with coining the word *robotics*) considered his robots to be unpredictable machines, capable of seemingly inexplicable acts due to contradictions in their programming.

Photo by Alex Gotfryd, courtesy of Doubleday

Real Robots

The robot family tree probably took root in the 18th century. It was at this time that Jacques de Vaucanson created and demonstrated a mechanical duck that was supposedly so lifelike that it drew gasps from those who saw it. Supposedly, the duck, which had 400 pieces in its wings alone, could swim, quack, eat, excrete, and perform a variety of other duck-like behaviors. Vaucanson also built two human-like machines, one of which played a flute and the other the drums, amazing feats when you consider how difficult it is to play a musical instrument.

In the late 18th century, Pierre and Henri-Louis Jaquet-Droz, father-and-son inventors, created three mechanical figurines named the Scribe, the Draftsman, and the Musician. These mechanical beings wrote letters, drew pictures, and played a small organ, respectively.

Unfortunately, by the time the 19th century rolled around, inventors had gone about as far as they could with their clever machines. The next generation in the family tree of robotics required some type of machine intelligence, a quality that was not forthcoming until the advent of computers.

Simple robots first appeared in 1961, when General Motors purchased a robot called Unimate to perform die-casting tasks. A company called Unimation manufactured Unimate. Unimate cost $18,000 and could learn and perform 180 steps, but was little more than a mechanical arm. A human controller guided the robot through each of its steps, with the robot recording each step along the way. After recording the steps, Unimate simply replayed them from memory. Because training the robot was so simple, it was easy to reprogram the robot to handle different tasks.

In spite of General Motor's success with Unimate, robotics garnered about as much respect as Rodney Dangerfield. Few companies thought industrial robots could enhance their production, especially considering that robots did nothing humans couldn't do.

Still, in the mid 1960s, scientists at Stanford, MIT, and SRI International began experimentation with robots that incorporated artificial intelligence and TV cameras to guide the arm. After much refinement, these new robots were actually capable of assembling items such as automobile water pumps, a complicated task that required the robot to sort through parts on a table and fit the parts together correctly.

By the 1970s, robots gained some credibility, but it wasn't until the 1980s that they came into their own. The automobile industry discovered that robots could take over many tedious or dangerous jobs, leaving the human workers to perform tasks that required more thought. For several years, the automobile industry represented a large market for robot manufacturers. In this period, other companies, such as IBM, Westinghouse, and General Electric, began building industrial robots. Figure 6.3 shows a typical robot.

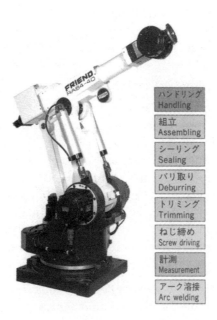

ハンドリング
Handling

組立
Assembling

シーリング
Sealing

バリ取り
Deburring

トリミング
Trimming

ねじ締め
Screw driving

計測
Measurement

アーク溶接
Arc welding

Figure 6.3.

Most robots are used today for industrial purposes.

Today, robots are still used extensively in auto manufacturing. Thanks to refinements in robot design, including robot sensors, increased accuracy, and better artificial intelligence routines, robots are used also for electronics and appliance assembly, when finer motor skills are required.

What Exactly Is a Robot?

Believe it or not, although you might think it is easy to define a robot, the folks who work in this field can't agree on just what a robot is. According to V. Daniel Hunt, author of *Understanding Robotics*, a robot is "a programmable multifunctional device designed to both manipulate and transport parts, tools, or specialized implements through variable programmed paths for the performance of specific manufacturing tasks." Because this definition is a mouthful, Hunt breaks the definition into seven characteristics that all robots share:

- *Programmable.* A robot should be able to store and execute programs, whether the program be on tape, floppy disk, or a computer chip.

- *Multifunctional.* A robot should be able to perform more than one type of task by executing different programs.

- *Manipulate.* A robot should be able to handle and manipulate objects in various ways, including gripping and rotating the objects with which it must work.

- *Transport.* A robot should be able to move itself or other objects from place to place.

- *Tools.* A robot should include tools for carrying out the operations it's programmed to perform.

- *Variable programmed paths.* A robot should be able to store and follow the sequential movements needed to complete its task.

- *Specific manufacturing tasks.* A robot should be able to complete its tasks without relying on human intervention and repeat the tasks exactly as required as often as necessary.

These preceding characteristics fit all the robots discussed so far. An assembly robot, for example, is multifunctional because you can program it to assemble more than one type of product. It is programmable because you can modify the steps of the assembly. An assembly robot can, of course, manipulate and transport parts during the assembly process, and, in order to assemble those parts, the robot requires tools. If this assembly robot is to be able to shuffle parts around, it's obviously capable of repeating sequential movements. Finally, this assembly robot performs its task repeatedly without human intervention.

If there's a problem with Hunt's definition, it's the inclusion of the word *manufacturing,* which limits the definition to industrial robots. As you'll see, robotics has advanced a great deal, even since 1990 when Hunt's book was published. Researchers are now studying robots intended for nonindustrial environments. Still, Hunt's definition surely fits 99 percent (or more) of the robots in existence. And, if you remove the word *manufacturing,* you can apply the definition to any robot.

An Excerpt From...

Intelligent Robotics by Mark H. Lee

Mark H. Lee, in his book *Intelligent Robotics,* provides a simpler definition for what he terms second-generation, or intelligent, robots. He says that an intelligent robotic device is a machine that "can manipulate physical objects in the real world, can sense events in the world, and is flexible." By flexible, Lee means "can change its task over time, both by being reprogrammed and by automatic task adaptation of some form." In spite of the new word *intelligent,* however, Lee still considers robots in an industrial environment only.

Robots and Sensory Input

One problem that has slowed advancements in robotics is the task of creating mechanisms that can accurately duplicate senses on a machine. The better a robot can sense and evaluate events in its environment, the more autonomous the robot becomes. The interaction of senses required to perform even the simplest actions, however, is much more complicated than most people realize.

Consider, for example, what happens when you try to pick up an egg. First, you focus your eyes on the egg and, using visual cues, extend your arm in the egg's direction. As your arm moves toward the egg, your eyes continually inform you of the closing distance between your hand and the egg. When you see that your hand is near the egg, you close your fingers to grasp it.

Your fingers then transmit tactile information, informing you whether you are gripping the egg tight enough to pick it up. This tactile sense is critical. If you exert too little pressure on the egg, it falls when you attempt to raise it. On the other hand, too much pressure causes you to crush the egg's delicate shell. Finally, as you raise your arm, the pressure of the egg in your hand, as well as the load on your arm, tells you how much lifting force is required. Too little force, and you cannot pick up the egg. Too much, and you throw the egg against the ceiling (see Figure 6.4).

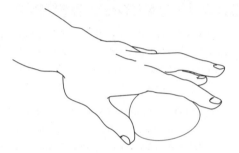

Figure 6.4.

The simple act of picking up an egg is much more complex than you might suspect.

Although the capability to duplicate all five basic senses would be useful in robotics, only three—touch, hearing, and sight—are the basis for robot sensors used today. It's not unreasonable, however, to imagine robots that could employ an artificial olfactory sense to sniff out particles in the air or a taste sense for evaluating liquids, powders, and other similar materials. Currently, though, robot sensors are limited to five types: tactile, range, proximity, acoustic, and visual.

Tactile Sensors

Tactile sensors can tell a robot whether it's touching an object, how tightly it's gripping the object, the shape of the object, and whether an object is slipping from its grasp. Although this sensing power might at first seem amazing, in practice it is actually fairly simple. For example, a touch sensor might comprise only a single micro switch that triggers when a robot's hand closes over an object. Switches capable of producing analog signals, on the other hand, can indicate the amount of pressure applied to an object by transmitting larger values for stronger forces.

Many robot gripping surfaces use a *sensor array,* which is a group of individual tactile elements, any of which can be activated at a given time. By examining the values returned by the array, a robot can determine whether an object is slipping, and, depending on the sensitivity of the sensor, even the rough shape of the object. Currently, researchers are studying special conductive *elastomer sheets* to use as robot skin. This material can sense not only contact, but also infrared radiation, magnetic fields, and sound waves.

Range and Proximity Sensors

Range sensors determine the distance between the sensor and the target object, whereas proximity sensors determine the presence of specific objects. The main difference between the two is that range sensors usually measure longer distances.

In any case, both types of sensors use similar methods of distance detection. Light detectors, for example, measure light reflected from an object, whereas magnetic detectors determine the presence of metals. Acoustic sensors, similar to those used in ultrasound machines, measure sound waves to determine distances. Lasers, too, can perform range detection. Obviously, some methods are better for long-range detection than others. Light detectors, for example, have a longer effective range than magnetic detectors.

Such sensors are frequently used to guide robot arms within specific distances of objects, much the same way your eyes guide your hand when you reach for something. In fact, if you had proximity sensors in your fingertips, you could pick up an egg with your eyes closed. If you find this hard to imagine, think about reaching toward a hot stove with your eyes closed. You don't have to touch the stove to know when you're getting too close!

Acoustic Sensors

I have already mentioned acoustic sensors in the preceding section, "Range and Proximity Sensors." Acoustic sensors can be used also for determining surface traits, object dimensions, and object shapes. Acoustic sensors incorporate a transmitter that generates ultrasonic sound waves (see Figure 6.5). A computer can then translate the waves that bounce from objects into pictures of objects.

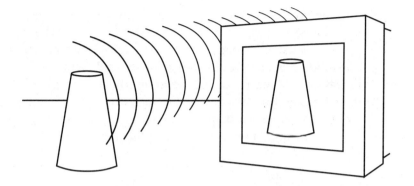

Figure 6.5.

Acoustic sensors can use sound waves to formulate pictures.

Suppose, for example, that an assembly robot is looking for a part. Its acoustic sensor can scan the work area, creating pictures that the robot can compare with shapes in its memory. When the robot makes a match, it picks up the part and continues with the assembly.

Visual Sensors

Machine vision systems are among the most sophisticated sensors a robot can have. Because visual feedback allows robots to become more autonomous, a great deal of research focuses on reproducing this sense. When you realize that humans retrieve more information about their environment through the eyes than through any other sense organ, you'll understand why scientists view machine vision as so important.

At the moment, however, the applications for machine vision are limited. They are used mostly for locating, identifying, and counting. Even within this narrow field of utility, however, limitations exist. For example, only a small number of objects are included in the machine's visual field. In addition, the objects must be well lit and cannot overlap.

Still, machine vision is especially useful for inspection tasks, including checking object shapes and counting. Robots with visual sensors also can handle certain types of monitoring tasks. In some cases, machine vision is more reliable than human vision. For example, a person inspecting a long run of color samples might be unable to identify subtle changes in color, whereas a robot equipped with machine vision can easily detect minute changes.

Although there are many types of machine vision systems, most incorporate a television-type camera (see Figure 6.6). The camera produces an analog image which is converted into a digital image. The robot then analyzes the digital image using template matching or feature analysis. In *template matching,* the robot compares the digital image with images stored in memory. In *feature analysis,* the robot checks for such shape characteristics as dimension, area, orientation, and other distinguishing features.

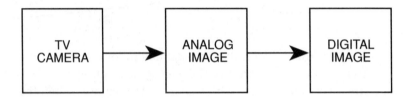

Producing images and translating them into digital form is easy. However, interpreting the digital images is the subject of much artificial intelligence research. (Neural networks and genetic algorithms, which you read about in Chapter 3, are sometimes used for this interpretation task.) As you can well imagine, the interpretation of image data is even more critical in systems incorporating *three-dimensional* machine vision, which enables robots to determine spatial relationships.

Robots and A-Life

If industrial robots were the end of the robot line, there would be little reason to include robots in a book on a-life. However, advances in robotics have paved the way for fascinating machines that are, in many ways, artificial life forms. These types of robots currently have little industrial value. Applications for home, military, and space, however, abound.

Imagine, for example, a little robotic critter that scampers around your house vacuuming the floor. Or how about a squad of insect-like machines capable of exploring the surface of a distant planet. Today's robotics technology is closer than ever to producing such machines.

Hundreds of scientists are currently working in the field of robotics, many of which are trying to create more effective means of duplicating human intelligence on a machine. Although the results of these studies are valuable, there's not much about them here; you already read about AI in Chapter 5, "The Silicon Brain: Artificial Intelligence." One researcher, however, stands out from the rest due to his radical views on AI and its applicability to robotics.

Bugs!

One of the more unconventional researchers in the field of robotics is MIT's Rodney Brooks (Figure 6.7). Brooks and his team of graduate students created a squad of robot insects that may someday evolve into tiny machines capable of doing various chores from cleaning the house to exploring new worlds. But Brooks' claim to fame is not so much what his robots do, but how they go about doing it. Frustrated by the overwhelming difficulties of trying to run complex artificial intelligence routines on robots, Brooks looked to insects for inspiration. He reasoned that insects, after all, can outperform even the most sophisticated robots. Moreover, they do it without relying on complex calculations.

This line of inquiry led Brooks to his bottom-up theory of building complex behaviors. Rather than trying to cram reams of symbolic knowledge into an artificial brain to make a robot functional, Brooks decided it made more sense to start with basic behaviors and use them as building blocks for more complex behaviors. In other words, he believes you must teach a robot to stand before you teach it to run.

Subsumption Architecture

As you might have guessed, Brooks, who is known for his radical ideas about artificial intelligence, threw to the wind most conventional AI paradigms and set off on his own path. Brooks believes that the way to create useful robots is not to imbue them with human-like intelligence, but rather to provide them with a series of simple behaviors that work together to complete a task. Using what Brooks calls *subsumption architecture,* his mechanical insects operate by reflexive responses to external stimuli.

Figure 6.7.

Rodney Brooks shown with Hannibal, one of the robot lab's newest creations.

Photo by Bruce Frisch

How is this different from more conventional approaches to robot intelligence? The traditional approach is to create in the robot's mind a model of the world in which it must operate. To function in this environment, the robot matches objects in its field of vision to templates stored in its memory. To move from place to place, for example, the robot must locate possible exits (which requires a lot of shape matching and analyzing) and consult its map to determine where the exit leads. If the exit doesn't go where the robot wants to go, it looks for another possible exit (see Figure 6.8). All this processing eats up a lot of computing time.

Brooks' approach is to provide his robots with a hierarchy of named behaviors like Track Prey, Move Forward, Back Off, and Lift Leg. The top of the hierarchy represents the robot's goal (for example, Track Prey), with more basic behaviors represented in lower levels (such as Lift Leg). When one of Brooks' robots is on the prowl, it doesn't consult an electronic map, match object shapes, or perform other complex calculations; it simply moves. When something comes between the robot and its goal, a new behavior takes over, or *subsumes,* the current behavior until the crisis is solved, at which point the original behavior regains control.

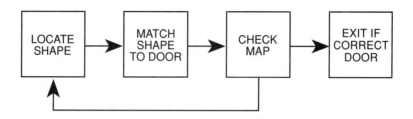

Figure 6.8.

The traditional approach to robot intelligence involves intensive computations.

For example, suppose a robot is performing its Track Prey behavior. The robot begins to Move Forward toward the prey. But before reaching the prey, it bumps into a low obstacle on the floor. The Lift Leg behavior subsumes the Move Forward behavior, allowing the robot to climb onto the obstacle. Once the leg is up, Move Forward again takes over, and the robot starts to climb. The shift in weight, however, triggers the Rotate Joints behavior, which subsumes Move Forward until the robot has gained firm footing.

One advantage of this "brainless" approach to robot intelligence is that it requires only a minimal amount of computing power to handle the simple behaviors. Thus, robots based on Brooks' designs are much smaller and cheaper than robots that require sophisticated computers to function.

Another advantage of Brooks' subsumption architecture is the ease with which more complex behaviors can be built into a robot. There's no need for a central intelligence to understand everything that's going on in the machine. The robot's designer just adds simple behaviors until the robot can do what it needs to do. Moreover, the complex interaction of the many simple behaviors often leads to *emergent behaviors,* behaviors that are not explicitly programmed, but occur spontaneously.

Meet the Beetles

The robots created by Brooks' team vary in shape, size, and function, from Herbert, who gathers soda cans from desktops, to Squirt, a mechanical roach about the size of a grasshopper. With such intimidating names as Genghis and Attila, Brooks' more famous mechanical bugs (designed in part by graduate student Colin Angle) roam around a room, navigating obstacles and sometimes even stalking human beings. Their behavior is surprisingly complex for brainless machines.

Genghis, who looks like an ant from the Twilight Zone, sports six legs, six eyes, and two whiskers on its foot-long mechanical body (see Figure 6.9). Its infrared eyes sense the presence of new prey (people), and after finding the prey, Genghis begins to stalk slowly but relentlessly. But what makes Genghis special is the way it teaches itself to walk, thanks to programming added by computer scientist Pattie Maes, another member of Brooks' team. When one first activates Genghis, it has no idea how to coordinate its legs. Through trial and error, however, it manages first to stand and then finally to creep forward. (Recently, Colin Angle started a company called I.S. Robotics, which sells a production model of Genghis for research and educational uses—see Figure 6.10.)

Figure 6.9.

Genghis is a talented robot that can teach itself to walk.

Photo by Bruce Frisch

Attila, which is a refined version of Genghis and to whom Brooks refers as "the world's most complex robot," weighs only three and a half pounds, but still manages to hold 150 sensors, 23 motors, and 10 microprocessors in its small body. Thanks to its impressive hardware array, Attila can outperform Genghis by navigating over larger obstructions and even scampering up steep inclines. The newest version of Attila, dubbed Hannibal, is shown in Figure 6.11. Several of Brooks' robots are pictured in Figure 6.12.

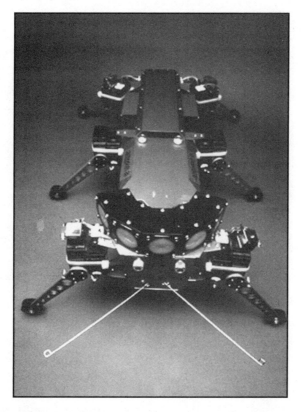

Photo by Bruce Frisch

Figure 6.10.

I.S. Robotic's production version of Genghis.

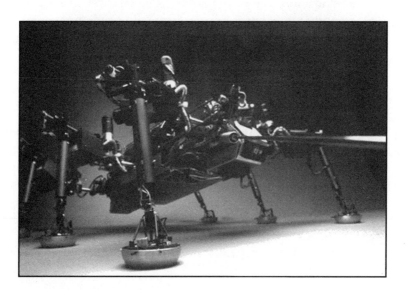

Figure 6.11.

Hannibal is one of the most complex robots ever built.

Photo by Bruce Frisch

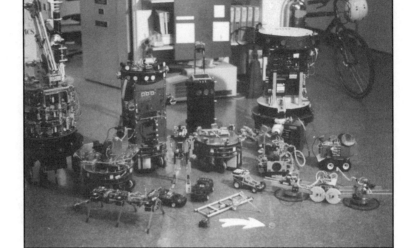

Figure 6.12.

The many robots created by Brooks and his team.

Photo courtesy of MIT

Although Genghis, Attila, and Hannibal are much smaller than most conventional robots, they are giants compared with the gnat-sized robots research scientist Anita Flynn envisions for the future. Flynn and Brooks have already created a robot insect about the size of a grasshopper. This timid creature, called Squirt, propels itself around a room on tiny wheels (see Figure 6.13). Its hardware comprises only one microprocessor, one motor, two sound sensors, one light sensor, and two batteries, yet Squirt acts much like a timid insect, hiding in the shadows and emerging only when the room is quiet. Squirt's successor, ironically named Goliath, is another of the lab's tiny robots, and is, in fact, now the lab's tiniest autonomous microrover (Figure 6.14).

Brooks is positive that his subsumption architecture is the best way to create usable robots. He's so sure, in fact, that he continually annoys his colleagues by insisting that their studies of AI will lead to a dead end. Perhaps Brooks is right. Perhaps he's not. Perhaps future robot designs will incorporate ideas from both paradigms. One thing is for sure: Brooks' robots work.

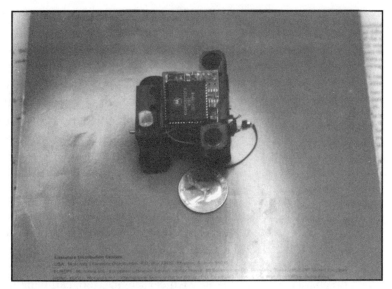

Photo courtesy of MIT

Figure 6.13.

Squirt likes to hide
in the dark.

Photo by Bruce Frisch

Figure 6.14.

Goliath is now the
robot lab's tiniest
robotic insect.

The Future of Robotics

Robots today perform only limited functions in highly structured environments. Because robots deal poorly with unpredictable situations, they are far from replacing humans in the work force. However, with continual advances in robot sensors and artificial intelligence, the goal of an automated manufacturing facility may be realized before too long. Machine vision and mobility are the two areas that need the greatest advancement before we can reach this goal—they are the key elements in producing autonomous robots.

But the study of robotics reaches way beyond the confines of the industrial complex. Advances in robotics will lead to advances in many other related fields as well. For example, how about a robotic car that can safely transport cargo (including people) with virtually no chance of an accident? Medical science, too, can benefit from robotics through the creation of artificial organs. Research has already pointed the way to fully functional artificial hearts. Assuming that advances continue, a time might come when artificial parts can replace virtually every part of the human body. Immortality anyone?

People have long dreamed of building robot servants dedicated to providing a person's every whim. Although such full-function robots are a long way in the future, robots designed to handle specific tasks are already here. Transitions Research Corporation, for example, built a prototype robotic nurse (see Figure 6.15). Dubbed HelpMate, this mechanical hospital helper delivers meals to hospital beds. Future versions of HelpMate, however, might navigate from floor to floor in a large hospital, shuffling medical records, pharmaceuticals, blood samples, and other medical needs from one department to another.

Human versus Machine

Hans Moravec, a researcher at Carnegie Mellon's Field Robotics Center and author of the books *Mind Children: The Future of Robot and Human Intelligence* and *The Age of the Mind: Transcending the Human Condition Through Robots,* believes that robots imbued with fully human intelligence will be common within 50 years.

According to Moravec, intelligent robots "looking quite unlike the machines we know will explode into the universe, leaving us behind in a cloud of dust."

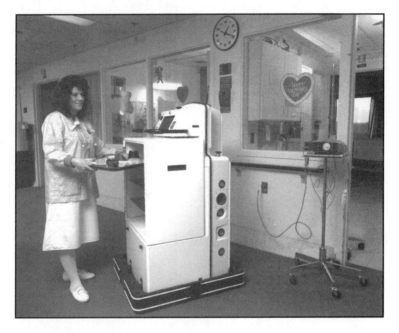

Photo courtesy of Transitions Research Corp

Figure 6.15.

In the near future, robotic servants like HelpMate will handle routine tasks such as delivering a meal to a hospital bed.

Leaving us behind? What happened to the idea that robots were meant to serve humankind? Could robots designed solely to assist us actually become a dominant race? Moravec believes so. In fact, Moravec theorizes that, to have any hope of keeping up with these self-evolving machine intelligences, humans might have to leave their bodies behind, transferring their minds into supercomputers (see Figure 6.16).

No Exterminators Needed

Rodney Brooks' view of the future is not quite so grim. He doesn't worry about artificially intelligent beings taking over the universe; he feels there's no need to give robots human intelligence in the first place. As his subsumption architecture demonstrates, robots can be useful when given an intelligence only on a par with an insect's.

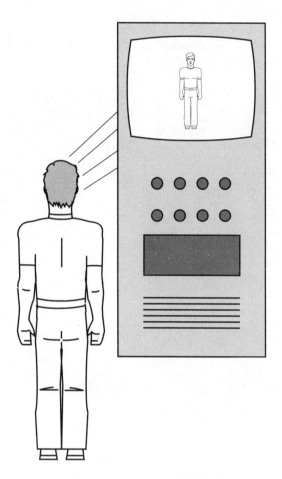

Figure 6.16.

Humans might have to leave their bodies behind and transfer their minds into supercomputers.

In fact, Brooks sees these insect-like robots becoming smaller and smaller, even to the point that doctors can inject them into the human bloodstream to repair clogged arteries. On a larger scale, he says that humankind will mass-produce gnat-sized robots by using similar techniques used to manufacture computer chips. These tiny robots will come in many varieties, each designed to perform a specific task. Thousands of "gnatbots," for example, might dwell in your carpet, constantly searching for and removing particles of dirt. Another type of gnatbot might swarm over your lawn, chewing your grass down to a predetermined height.

Although gnatbots won't be at your local J.C. Penney any time soon, scientists are already making advances in the creation of tiny motors carved from a silicon chip and controlled by piezoelectric crystals. Thanks to such technology, Anita Flynn believes we'll soon see millimeter-sized computer chips that can get up and walk.

Conclusion

Will future robots enable the human race to enjoy a more carefree and secure life than ever before? Or will our creations turn on us in unexpected ways, taking away the freedom we strove to gain and relegating us to the biological trash bin? As we gain access to the secrets of life, we become capable of engineering any future imaginable. But only by staying alert can we hope to remain in control.

Worlds of Imagination: Virtual Reality

Buster Babbage wasn't much of a warrior. His sword techniques were sloppy, his reflexes were slow, and he spent far too much time in the local pubs. So, today, as he stood on the surface of the moon with only a dagger, his leather armor, and his alcohol-blurred wits, he wondered why his so-called buddy, Stu, had talked him into coming here. The moon didn't look like a very cool place. In fact, it looked downright dangerous.

"Hey, twit. Is that Lunar Lynx flop I smell, or did your mommy forget to change your diaper?"

Buster spun around to face the source of the voice. What he saw nearly stunned him blind. The creature, which leaned against a rocky outcrop nonchalantly picking its teeth with a dagger, looked like some reject from a genetics lab. Its bulbous, purple head oozed green fluid, its jet black eyes glared hatred, and the teeth...Buster wondered "Are those things really teeth?"

The creature grinned and advanced, tossing its dagger from hand to hand. Buster glanced at his own dagger and groaned. The situation was getting out of hand. He wouldn't last a minute against this...this...*thing*.

Buster turned to run, but the creature attacked. It crashed into Buster like a runaway meteor, driving him down to the lunar surface, crushing his face into sharp rocks and abrasive meteor dust. The creature was heavy, but Buster managed to squirm around just in time to see the thing's dagger plunge toward his face.

"I want out!" Buster yelled. "I want out *now!*"

The words barely out of Buster's mouth, the moonscape began to shimmer and shift, finally dissolving into a universe of twinkling white dots. Buster squeezed his eyes shut, driving back the dizziness. When he opened his eyes, Stu was already unbuckling him from the SimSuit.

"Man," Stu grumbled, "you're such a wimp! I beat that level weeks ago."

If this scenario sounds like something from a science fiction story set in the year 2593, you'd better take a deep breath before you read on. Virtual reality (VR) is almost upon us, and there's little doubt that, if nothing else, it'll revolutionize the entertainment industry. The day will come when you'll go to a theater not to watch a movie, but to participate in it.

Someday, you'll be able to ride a bike through the sky with E.T. perched on the handle bars, creep through a demon-infested house in the latest Clive Barker movie, or even go on a quest with King Arthur's knights.

Of course, the applications for VR go way beyond the entertainment industry. Using VR, you might someday be able to learn to fly a plane without ever leaving the ground. You might, in fact, be able to pilot a ship to Mars. The possibilities for realistic training simulations are unlimited. The business world, too, will enjoy such advantages as virtual conferences, in which people from around the

world can instantly meet in a computer-generated conference room. In fact, once VR takes hold, it'll likely change the world in more ways than one can imagine.

What is virtual reality? That's a question I'll discuss in some depth in this chapter. But as is typical with new technologies, virtual reality means different things to different people. Basically, virtual reality is a new way to communicate through computers. Instead of communicating using text and static pictures, as is typical with computers, VR communicates with as many of the human senses as possible. VR means taking people inside the communication channel, instead of leaving them outside looking in (Figure 7.1).

Figure 7.1.

VR means taking people inside the communication channel, instead of leaving them outside, looking in.

For example, you've probably used your computer to "talk" to other users in an online conference. In such a conference, when you type words on-screen, your computer instantly transmits them through the telephone lines to every other user in the conference. It's a lot like talking with your fingers. In a VR conference, though, you would do no typing. Instead, you would find yourself in a computer-generated room talking face-to-face with the other people in the conference. Although you would see, hear, and possibly even touch the other conference participants, they are not in the room. They are located anywhere on the planet, linked to you only through high-speed communications lines.

Of course, a VR conference such as this is still a long way from becoming a reality. For one, data transmission speeds are currently nowhere near fast enough to transmit the huge amounts of graphics, sound, and other sensory data involved. If you've ever run a program like a flight simulator on your computer, you know what I mean. Even a fast computer struggles to update the screen display speedily enough to simulate a volatile 3-D world. And a computer can handle data astronomically faster than a telephone line can transmit data.

Although it might be some time before you can participate in a virtual conference, there are already VR systems in existence that can provide amazingly realistic experiences. How do these VR systems work? Read on and see.

Concepts of Virtual Reality

People perceive the world by using their brains to interpret the huge amount of data provided by their senses. The images you see; the sounds you hear; the objects you touch, taste, and smell, all combine to build, in your brain, a detailed model of your surroundings.

When an infant comes into the world, this flood of sensory information has no meaning. The infant has no understanding of up and down, of hot and cold, of light and dark. It's only through experience that the infant learns to relate the images, sounds, and other sensory data with which it's confronted to her new world. This amazing learning process proceeds rapidly. Within a year or two, the infant has gained a basic understanding of the way the world works. By the time this child is four or five years old, the rules of the physical world are permanently etched into her brain.

This association between sensory data and the world in which you live is so powerful that you have almost no control over it. When

presented with artificially generated sensory data, no matter how hard you try, you simply cannot stop your brain from making the interpretations it has been so meticulously trained to make (Figure 7.2). Imagine watching a movie filmed in first-person viewpoint of a roller coaster speeding over its track. Even though you know you're not moving, even though you know you're safe in your seat, you experience the same dizzying disorientation you might feel if you were actually riding that roller coaster. You might even experience motion sickness.

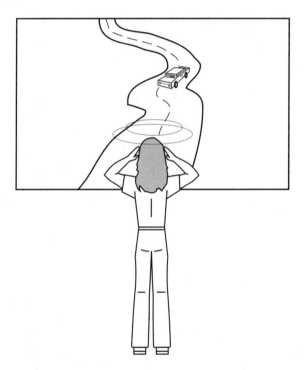

Figure 7.2.

The association between your senses and the world around you is so strong that you have almost no control over it.

In a way, that roller coaster movie is actually a simple VR experience. By showing the images you'd see while riding a roller coaster, the movie pulls you from your seat and into the film. In order for the illusion to be complete, however, it must stimulate as many of your senses as possible. To be fully effective, VR systems apply four basic concepts to the VR experience: viewpoint, navigation, manipulation, and immersion.

Viewpoint

Viewpoint in VR is simply the simulated position of your eyes in a virtual world (Figure 7.3). Obviously, for the VR system to display what you see, it must know where you are located in the virtual world and in which direction you're facing. If the viewpoint is wrong, the entire VR experience is confusing.

Figure 7.3.

Viewpoint is the position of your eyes in a virtual world.

For example, suppose you start your car, thinking it's in reverse when it's actually in first gear. You turn in your seat, look out the back window, and give the car a little gas. Rather than moving backward, though, your car leaps forward. Makes you feel a little strange, doesn't it? For a second or two, you are completely disoriented. This is the type of experience you'd have if a VR system had an incorrect viewpoint.

For a VR experience to be realistic, the viewpoint must be accurately located and continually updated to reflect new positions in the virtual world. When you turn your head left, you'll expect to have the scene shift appropriately (which means shifting the images to the right). When you look up, you'll expect to see more of the sky, not more of the ground. This shifting of viewpoints is called navigation.

Navigation

Navigation is the act of moving your viewpoint from one position to another in a VR environment (Figure 7.4). When you move your viewpoint, the computer must be capable of displaying new images based on your new position. When you think about it, this capability requires a tremendous amount of image processing. After all, even a minute shift of viewpoint changes everything you see to some extent. The relative position and angle of every object in your field of vision must be recalculated and the new images drawn. The process of navigation places the most strain on a VR graphics display.

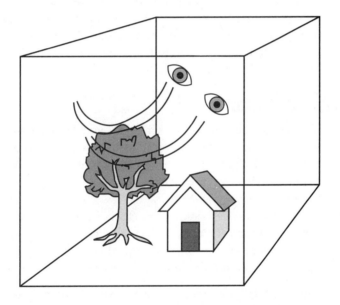

Figure 7.4.

Navigation is the act of moving around a virtual world.

To complicate matters, because a VR environment is a 3-D world, viewpoints must shift such that an object is viewed from any angle, including from in front of the object or from behind the object. Therefore, all objects in a VR environment must, like the world in which they appear, be 3-D objects. The computer constructs these 3-D objects by piecing together many flat surfaces, much like the facets on a jewel. The more surfaces required to build an object, the harder it is for the computer to update the image. This is because the computer has to run the old coordinates of each surface through a series of complex calculations to determine the new coordinates.

You now know why flight simulators feature such unrealistic and poorly detailed graphics displays. It's simply not possible for today's desktop computers to handle the immense amount of graphics data required for a detailed display and still keep the program running at a realistic speed. The more the computer is loaded down with graphics data, the slower it updates the screen display. In the worst case, the screen animation is so bogged down that what you see is more like a series of snapshots than a smoothly moving viewpoint.

Despite the huge number of calculations required to update a 3-D graphics display when a shift of viewpoint occurs, the computations involved have been refined over years to work as quickly as today's computers allow. In fact, when only the effects of viewpoint and navigation need be considered, VR systems today can provide an amazing visual experience, even though the objects in the VR environment are not as detailed as those in real life.

Manipulation

Thanks to viewpoint and navigation, you can step inside a VR environment and move around at will. Wherever you look or move, the computer generates a new display that reflects your new position in the VR world. However, this type of VR environment is a world frozen in time. Nothing moves. Every object is glued in place, suspended between ticks of the clock. In short, you can look, but you can't touch. Through object *manipulation,* however, your hands can join your eyes in the virtual world (Figure 7.5). You can, for example, reach out and pluck an object off a table.

In many ways, manipulation is like viewpoint. When you pick up an object and move it toward you, the object's position relative to your viewpoint is changing. That is, moving an object toward you is not unlike your moving toward the object. The main difference is that only the object you're manipulating changes. The remaining objects in the VR world are unaffected. In fact, if the object you are manipulating were the only object in the VR world, there would be virtually no difference between manipulation and changing viewpoint.

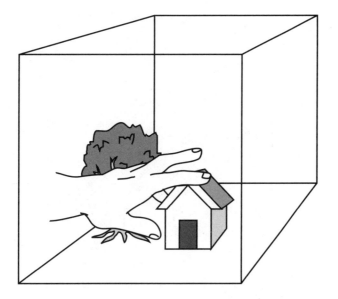

Figure 7.5.

Manipulation is the act of interacting with objects in a virtual world.

You might think this would make object manipulation easy to implement. But consider that the object being manipulated is moving to a new location in the VR world. This means that the computer must both shift the object's coordinates in the world *and* calculate the effect of that change on what you see. And what if your viewpoint is changing at the same time you are moving the object? For example, suppose you're following the object with your eyes as it moves toward you. The object's position must be recalculated, the change in the display due to that new position must be calculated, and then your new viewpoint also must be calculated. As you can see, manipulation is a much more complex procedure than you might at first believe.

Immersion

Viewpoint, navigation, and manipulation all work together to enable you to view and change the images you see in a VR environment. However, it is the quality of the immersion that makes you feel as if you're there. *Immersion* is the extent to which you are drawn into the VR world (Figure 7.6). If immersion could be quantified, it would be the measure of how realistic the simulation is.

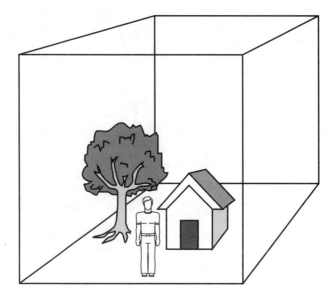

Figure 7.6.

When fully immersed in a virtual world, you feel as though you're actually there.

For example, when you watch your favorite TV show, although you might become involved in the story line, there's little doubt in your mind that you're sitting at home on your sofa. This is because the amount of immersion you're experiencing is low. When you glance away from the TV, you don't see Roseanne's living room or other members of Arsenio's studio audience. Instead, you see the door to your kitchen, the speakers of your stereo, or maybe little Stephen playing on the floor. In one quick glance, you've left the TV world and rejoined your own.

But, imagine glancing to your left, and instead of seeing your own home, you are seeing some strange guy in a Grateful Dead T-shirt jumping up from his seat and cheering Arsenio's next guest. You look behind you, and you see the rest of the studio audience. In fact, no matter how you turn your head, you see exactly what you'd see if you were actually sitting in that studio audience. Now, you're truly immersed in the experience. As far as you can tell, the real world has disappeared. All that you can see are the images presented to you by the computer controlling the VR environment.

Of course, by the time VR technology has advanced to the point in which it can plop you down into Arsenio Hall's audience, Arsenio will have been long off the air. Still, using today's technology, the

quality of visual and aural immersion is quite high. Although the objects you view in the VR world are not as finely detailed as a TV picture, they seem to be real, solid objects.

Fooling the Senses

Obviously, for a VR environment to be convincing, your senses must be fooled like they've never been fooled before. Although people have five basic senses, VR can create a realistic illusion by stimulating only sight and hearing. Luckily, these two senses are the ones which current VR systems are best equipped to stimulate. The next important sense is touch, which is extremely difficult to stimulate in a VR environment. It requires bulky suits, clumsy handwear, and heavy boots. And, in spite of all this hardware, VR can stimulate only simple touch sensations.

Sight

As you know from the roller coaster/movie example, fooling your eyes is not particularly difficult and can result in a stunning effect. Why are people so vulnerable to visual trickery? Because your eyes give you more information about the world than any other sense organ (Figure 7.7). In fact, the quality of immersion in a VR environment hinges mainly on the visual element. No matter how effectively sound, touch, taste, and smell are used in a VR world, without realistic visuals, the entire simulation falls flat on its virtual face.

As I wrote before, to create realistic visuals, the scenes you see in the virtual world must change when you move your viewpoint, usually by turning your head. One way movie theaters have done this is by surrounding the audience with screens, each screen acting as a window to the virtual world. When you look forward, you see the scene moving toward you. When you look to the side, you see the scene moving past. When you look behind, you see the scene moving away. The effect is so realistic that often even closing your eyes doesn't erase the illusion of movement.

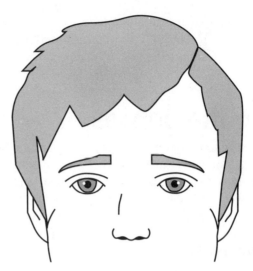

Figure 7.7.

Vision tells you more about the world than any other sense.

Don't believe it? Take a trip to Universal Studios in California or Florida. On one of the tour rides, your tram goes through a rotating tunnel, the inside of which is painted with a spiral pattern. The rotating spiral makes the tram seem to rotate in the opposite direction of the tunnel's rotation, a gut-wrenching effect. (The idea is that the tram is caught in an avalanche.) Closing your eyes isn't enough to immediately convince your brain that you're not rotating. It takes five or 10 seconds for your brain to switch from visual cues to other sensory cues. Until then, your mind stubbornly insists that you're rotating. Rides such as Star Tours at MGM Studios in Florida and Body Wars at Epcot Center, also in Florida, often have similar effects on people.

A simple VR system can create a similar illusion by using a headset that places a small viewing screen in front of each eye (Figure 7.8). When you move your head, the headset transmits movement data to the computer, which then uses the data to change your viewpoint and create the appropriate images on the screens. The effect is much like viewing the world through a diver's helmet.

Unfortunately, although the effect of both these visual techniques is realistic in a limited way, they are still a long way from reproducing the full visual effect of standing inside a virtual world. One way to improve the illusion might be to combine the movie-theater method with the headset. In this case, the headset might fit entirely over your head like a helmet. The scene, based on your current

viewpoint, appears all around the inside of the helmet. When you move your head, the helmet signals the computer to update the images you see. Of course, the calculations that determine new images on a screen must be performed for each and every segment of the display every time you move. These calculations would require an immense amount of computing power.

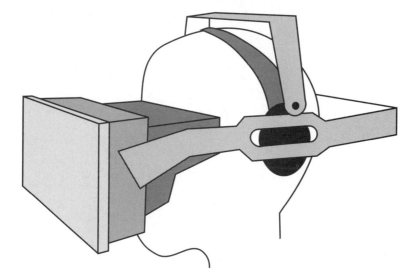

Figure 7.8.

Special headsets provide a view into a virtual world, as well as track the movement of the user's head.

Sound

Creating realistic sound in a VR world is a bit more complicated than it might initially seem. If you use stereo headphones, you know that you can move the position of a sound effect fairly easily, just by making the sound a little louder in one ear than in the other. The drawback to this technique is that the sound always stays "inside" your head, in an area somewhere between one ear and the other.

To create truly realistic sound, a VR system must be able to make sound effects sound as if they are coming from somewhere in the 3-D space of the virtual world. This might seem an impossible task, but recent studies on how humans detect the sources of sounds led to some interesting discoveries.

Just as you need two eyes to determine spatial relationships, so you need two ears to determine the direction of a sound in 3-D space. If someone drops a spoon directly in front of you, for example, the sound waves reach both of your ears at the same time. Your brain uses this information to determine that the sound came from in front. But if the spoon drops a bit to your left, the sound waves reach your left ear slightly before they reach your right ear. Again, your brain can translate this information into the direction of the sound (Figure 7.9).

Figure 7.9.

The delay between the time sound waves reach one ear and the other tells you the direction of the sound.

Touch

The most difficult sense to duplicate in a VR setting is touch, probably because our sense of touch can experience so many different types of sensations. Through touch, you can feel pressure, heat, cold, a variety of pain sensations, and even the weight of an object. As you learned in Chapter 6, "Silicon and Steel: The Study of Robotics," your brain generates a great deal of sensory information just by picking up an egg. Mechanically duplicating all these sensations is one of the toughest challenges VR researchers have faced.

There currently are a few glove-like devices that create a small range of touch sensations (Figure 7.10). One type of glove uses small air bladders that inflate and deflate to apply different amounts of pressure to parts of the hand. Another glove uses an arrangement of pistons to apply pressure to the fingers. Still another uses special wires that, when heated, simulate the feel of different textures. Although these first attempts at simulating the sense of touch are a step in the right direction, this element of VR has a long way to go before it'll be capable of providing a convincing illusion.

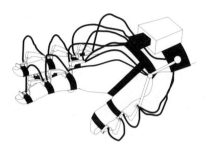

Figure 7.10.

Researchers have created different types of gloves to provide a sense of touch in VR systems.

VR and A-Life

What does all this have to do with a-life? In many ways, nothing. But consider the fictional scenario that started this chapter. The gruesome creature with which our hero grappled is an example of artificial life, at least to the extent that it physically looks alive, thinks intelligently, can carry on a conversation, and can react to the player's actions. Maybe this artificial creature can't reproduce (or maybe it can), but, as long as the player is immersed in the VR world, the creature seems to be alive in every reasonable way.

Again, current VR technology is nowhere near capable of producing such a creature. In fact, Buster's lunar opponent

The Convolvotron

A fter much research into the characteristics of sound waves, some clever scientists (Elizabeth Wenzel, Scott Foster, and Dr. Frederick Wightman) came up with complicated mathematical formulas that, when applied to a sound wave, can make the sound seem to come from any specific direction. The result of this work is a headset called the Convolvotron, a device that can create realistic sound for use in VR systems.

is not unlike that famous fictional computer, HAL 9000, that you read about earlier in this book. In both cases, the artificial intelligence routines used must be capable of controlling the a-life form's reactions to its environment in a logical and believable way. It'll be many years before such interaction is possible.

Still, current VR technology can create video game-type life forms capable of limited responses in specific situations. Although these creations cannot respond to random stimuli, they can provide a reasonable facsimile of life in a highly structured and predictable environment in similar ways that creatures depicted in computer video games do.

Desktop Virtual Reality

People use the term virtual reality pretty loosely these days. Just about any computer software that creates a 3-D world through which you can move calls itself virtual reality. A program that creates a virtual world on a computer screen is taking advantage of something called *desktop virtual reality*. Such software can be anything from a computer game to a VR authoring system. The latter enables you to create your own VR world without learning computer programming. On your book disk, in fact, is a program that Virtual Reality Studio 2.0 created. Virtual Reality Studio 2.0 is a VR authoring system. (To install the program, please see the last book page, facing the disk.)

When you have the program installed, run it by changing to the \ALIFE\VR directory, typing **VR**, and pressing Enter. (Note that this program must be run from drive C.) When the graphics appear on-screen, press Esc to reset the VR world. You then see the screen shown in Figure 7.11.

In the center of the screen is a window that looks out onto the virtual world. To move through the virtual world, click the buttons on the control panel near the bottom of the screen or press the appropriate key on your keyboard. To continue moving in a particular direction, click and hold the left mouse button on the appropriate button. Or, hold down the appropriate key on your keyboard.

Virtuality

I f you want an unpredictable opponent, how about competing against another human being in a VR environment? This is what happens in the VR arcade game, Virtuality, currently operating in video arcades in eight U.S. cities.

In Virtuality, two human opponents enter a VR world that looks much like a giant chess board. Once there, the players try to shoot each other, all the while avoiding a pterodactyl that can swoop down, grab a player, drag him up into the virtual sky, and then drop him back to the playing board. Sound like fun?

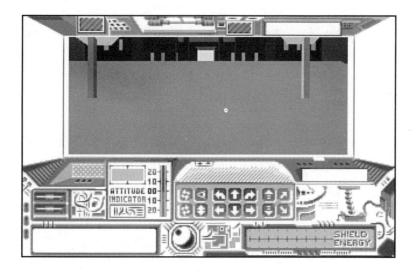

Figure 7.11.

*The main screen
of the desktop
virtual reality
demonstration
program.*

Table 7.1 lists the controls of the virtual reality program and what they do.

Table 7.1. The virtual reality demonstration program's controls and functions.

Control Button	Key	Function
⬆	O	Move forward
⬇	K	Move backward
⬅	H	Move left
➡	J	Move right
↰	Q	Turn left
↱	W	Turn right
⬆	R	Fly up
⬇	F	Fly down
↗	P	Look up
↘	L	Look down

141

continues

Table 7.1. Continued.

Control Button	Key	Function
	N	Rotate left
	M	Rotate right
	Esc	Reset VR world
	C	Turn off crosshair
	Shift-Ctrl-Esc	Exit the program

As you experiment with the movement controls, you'll see that you can fly around this VR world just about any way you like. No matter where you move, the screen shows the scene from your new viewpoint. If all this seems a little confusing, follow the pictorial "fly through" included as follows. (In all steps, pressing a control means placing the mouse pointer over the control and holding down the left mouse button, or holding down the appropriate key on the keyboard.)

1. Press the Fly Up control until you center the mansion in the view window as in Figure 7.12.

Figure 7.12.

2. Press the Move Forward control until you move onto the mansion's porch. See Figure 7.13.

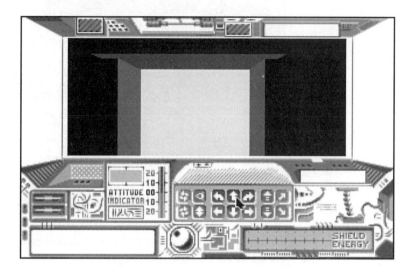

Figure 7.13.

3. Press the Move Backward control until you back up as far as possible. See Figure 7.14.

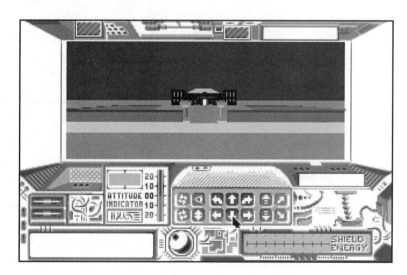

Figure 7.14.

4. Press the Fly Up control until the mansion is at the bottom of the view window, as shown in Figure 7.15.

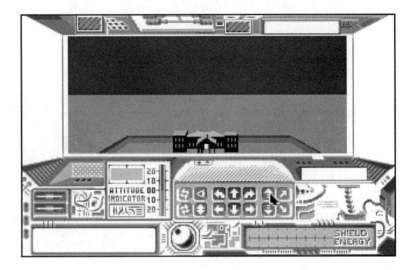

Figure 7.15.

5. Press the Look Down control until the mansion is at the top of the view window, as shown in Figure 7.16.

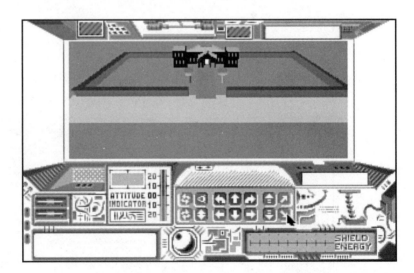

Figure 7.16.

6. Press the Fly Up control until you've flown as high as you can. See Figure 7.17.

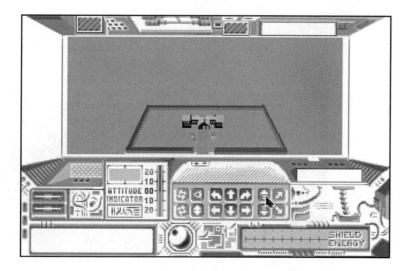

Figure 7.17.

7. Click the Reset control, or press Esc, to reset the VR world. See Figure 7.18.

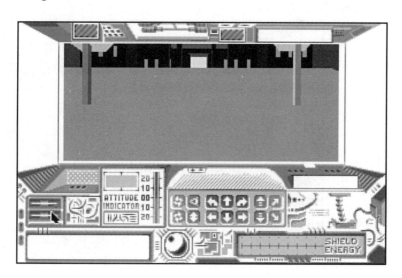

Figure 7.18.

8. Press the Fly Up control until you center the mansion in the view window. See Figure 7.19.

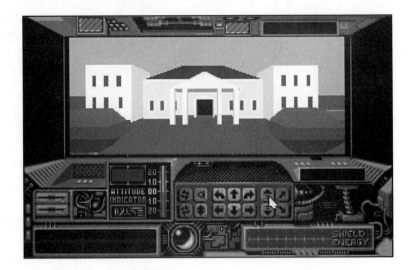

Figure 7.19.

9. Press the Move Forward control until you are near the mansion. See Figure 7.20.

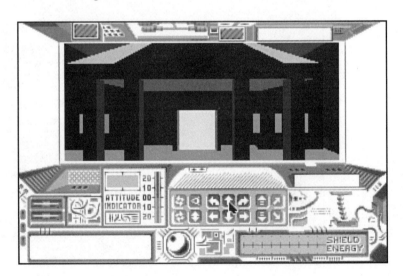

Figure 7.20.

10. Press the Turn Right control until you see the right wing of the mansion, as shown in Figure 7.21.

Figure 7.21.

11. Press the Turn Left control until you see the Left wing of the mansion, as shown in Figure 7.22.

Figure 7.22.

12. Continue experimenting with the controls to see the mansion from different viewpoints. Figure 7.23 shows one possible viewpoint.

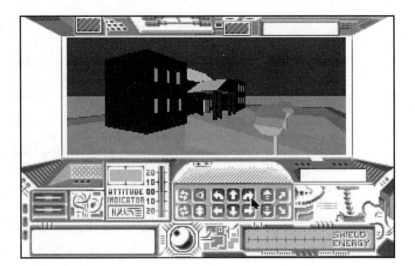

Figure 7.23.

Conclusion

By combining VR with a-life, someday it might be possible to create realistic virtual worlds populated with any type of creature you can imagine. These worlds might be modeled after our own reality and used for training or virtual travel, or they might be bizarre places, filled with creatures that previously existed only in our dreams. The possibilities are almost limitless.

If you'd like to see what a future VR system might be like, jog down to your local videotape store and rent a copy of *The Lawnmower Man*. This movie features some of the most breathtaking VR scenes ever filmed. But, although the VR environments shown in *The Lawnmower Man* are fascinating, VR's potential extends well beyond the realms of entertainment.

For example, you can use VR systems in 3-D CAD (computer-aided design) systems. These VR/CAD systems enable an engineer not only to construct a 3-D model on-screen, but also to "walk around" the model, examining it from any viewpoint. This design technique is especially helpful to architects, who can design entire buildings on a computer and walk through them before any actual construction begins.

Doctors, scientists, students, athletes, military personnel, artists, the handicapped—just about anybody is likely to see VR become a part of their lives in one form or another. And the time when VR touches your life might be a lot closer than you think.

A-Life Off the Shelf— Commercial A-Life Programs

In the course of reading this book, you have learned a lot about artificial life. Along the way, you looked behind the scenes at some of the techniques used to create a-life. You even explored some areas like expert systems and virtual reality, which, although might not directly qualify as a-life, are certainly associated with it. Hopefully, the programs on this book's disk give you a chance to see a-life in action and whet your appetite to know more about this intriguing area of computer science.

Luckily, the programs on this book's disk are only a tiny sample of the many programs with which you can experiment. Believe it or not, your local software store stocks some impressive examples of a-life, as well as various types of expert systems, desktop virtual reality packages, and other software that incorporate elements of a-life. In this chapter, you take a quick look at some top-notch software that can take you on further adventures in a-life.

SimAnt

The premiere publisher of commercial a-life programs is Maxis, which specializes in simulations, or *software toys,* as Maxis calls them. Maxis' first big hit was SimCity, which enabled the user to build and manage her own on-screen city. Although this package doesn't fall into the category of a-life, its success and the many awards it won paved the way for other impressive programs from Maxis. After SimCity, Maxis published many other simulations, most of which are related to a-life.

The simplest of these simulations is SimAnt, which is both an engrossing war game and a fascinating study of these ubiquitous insects. As you control the simulation, you decide where your ants dig their nests, how they scrounge up food, and even how and when they attack the dreaded red ants. If your colony manages to take over the entire backyard, they even get a shot at overrunning the house and making life miserable for the humans who live there.

Whether you choose the DOS or Windows version of SimAnt, the program organizes its display into various windows, menus, and dialog boxes. After you learn how to use the windows (thanks to the excellent manual, this takes only an hour or so), controlling the simulation is easy. For example, the Edit window (Figure 8.1) enables you to zoom in to the many tunnels that make up your nest. There, you see ants storing food and nurturing young. You even see new ants hatch from eggs.

On the other hand, the Surface View window (Figure 8.2) shows your ants scurrying from place to place on the surface as they gather food, battle enemies, and try to avoid spiders, ant lions, lawn mowers, and other fatal objects. If you want a bird's-eye view, the Map window gives you the lowdown on the current patch or displays the

entire backyard. To help you judge your ant-handling skills, bar graphs on the patches show the strengths of the black and red armies.

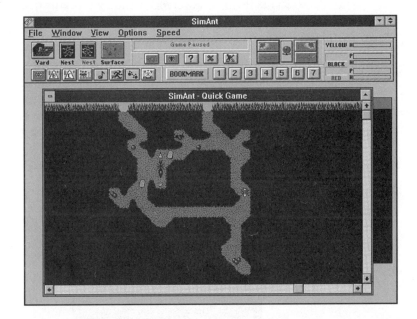

Figure 8.1.

SimAnt's Edit window enables you to see the tunnels that make up your nest.

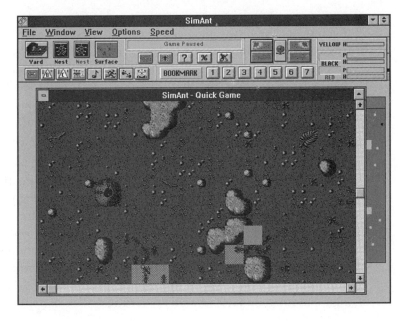

Figure 8.2.

The Surface View window shows your ants scurrying about their lives.

During a game, you can access many tools that control the ants and their universe. You might, for example, want to display the chemical scents that your ants leave behind as they explore their current area. These scents include *nest scents,* which guide ants back to the nest; *trail scents,* which guide ants to food; and *alarm scents,* which warn other ants of approaching danger.

In addition, the Caste control enables you to set the number of breeders, workers, and soldiers that are born into the nest, whereas the Behavior control determines how many ants stay to baby-sit the young, and how many hunt for food or dig new tunnels. Finally, to keep track of your progress, the History window (Figure 8.3) displays graphs of ant populations, food storage, colony health, and the number of ants eaten or killed.

Figure 8.3.

The History window displays helpful graphs.

If you're not interested in defeating the red ants, you can switch to SimAnt's experimental mode. Here, you begin with a patch containing small black-ant and red-ant nests, along with tools for manipulating the ants and their environment. The Barriers tool, for example, builds walls anywhere on the current patch, the Dig/Fill tool digs or fills in holes, and the Insecticide tool kills ants. Other tools include Add Food, Add Ants, and Drop Trails.

If you tire of experimenting and just want to sit back and learn about these pesky critters, you can access SimAnt's Information window (Figure 8.4), a hypercard-like database containing just about anything you might ever want to know about ants. With a quick click of your mouse, you can switch from card to card, whereas clicking highlighted words brings up a small window containing definitions. The cards that make up the Information window enable you to follow any line of inquiry you like, browsing interesting ant facts, as well as viewing dozens of pictures.

In short, SimAnt is a great way to experiment with a-life and to learn about ants and how they live. Older children are especially intrigued by this excellent simulation.

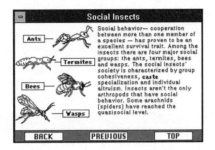

Social Insects

Social behavior— cooperation between more than one member of a species — has proven to be an excellent survival trait. Among the insects there are four major social groups: the ants, termites, bees and wasps. The social insects' society is characterized by group cohesiveness, caste specialization and individual altruism. Insects aren't the only arthropods that have social behavior. Some arachnids (spiders) have reached the quasisocial level.

Ants

Termites

Bees

Wasps

BACK   PREVIOUS   TOP

Figure 8.4.

SimAnt's Information window is a hypercard-like database.

SimLife

Although, in SimAnt, you can assign jobs to your ants and even decide what types of ants are born into your nest, you can't manipulate the critters at a genetic level. That is, using SimAnt you can experiment with a specific species of life, but you cannot create your own life or experiment with many different life forms— including both plants and animals—simultaneously. Maxis' SimLife, which is a much more complex simulation, gives you these almost God-like powers.

SimLife calls itself "an artificial life laboratory/playground designed to simulate environments, biology, evolution, ecosystems, and life." As such, the program features two main modes of operation. In the game mode, you select a specific scenario and then attempt to attain the scenario's goal. For example, in the Desert to Forest scenario, your task is to convert a desert world populated only with scrub into a lush forest world, whereas in the Feast and Famine scenario, you struggle to ensure the availability of food in an overpopulated world.

The scenarios test your knowledge of such important life-survival considerations as food chains, evolution, and genetics. But it is in SimLife's experimental mode that you spend the most time, dabbling with your world and the life forms in it, making changes to see how they affect the on-screen world. In this mode, you can set up simple experiments to study a specific life form or create an entire ecosystem in order to study the delicate balance required to sustain life.

Like SimAnt, SimLife organizes the immense amount of data it must display into separate windows that you can call up as needed. The Edit window (Figure 8.5) shows your world in a close-up view. It's on this window that you can add new plants or animals to your world or check on how specific life forms are doing. SimLife also has a Map window that provides a complete view of your world. You can set both the Edit and Map windows to display different types of information by setting the control panel to switch on altitude, moisture, soil depth, and other data displays.

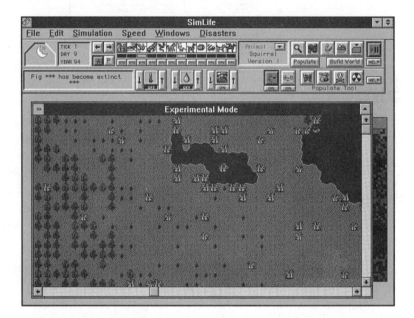

Figure 8.5.

SimLife's Edit window provides a close-up view of your world.

Although SimLife includes many ready-to-use plants and animals, there's nothing to stop you from playing the mad doctor and creating your own in SimLife's biology lab (Figure 8.6). In the lab, you first set a basic type for your new plant or animal. You can even use the simple graphics editor to design a new image for your custom life form. After you've got the basics taken care of, you can manipulate your life form's complex *genome* (Figure 8.7) to fine-tune your plant and animal exactly as you want it. (A genome comprises all the life form's genes, which control the way the life form looks and acts.) It's this capability to manipulate a life form's genes that makes SimLife such an interesting tool for experimentation.

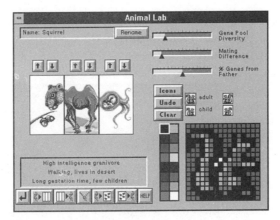

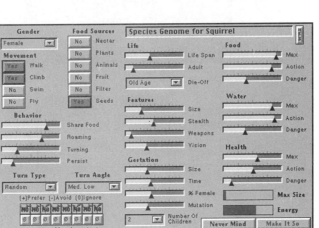

Figure 8.6.

The biology lab, which includes both the animal and plant labs, enables you to create your own life forms or edit existing ones.

Figure 8.7.

You can even manipulate a life form's genome, which includes genes for many of a plant's or animal's characteristics.

Not only can you manipulate the life forms in your world, but you can also modify the world itself. Using the World Design window (Figure 8.8), you can set such world characteristics as size, regional weather variation, average temperature, average moisture, and the number of rivers, lakes, and mountains. In addition, you can place toxins, which destroy life forms that consume them; mutagens, which cause mutations; universal food sources, which provide unlimited food for any species of animal; and barriers, which are like rock walls that life forms cannot pass.

After you have your world running, you have to keep track of all the activity. Using the various information windows, you can keep tabs on species diversity, mortality, and population, as well as call up various graphs. In addition, you can display detailed information

on the food web or the gene pool. For example, by inspecting the
Food Web information window (Figure 8.9), you can see which life
forms are consuming others.

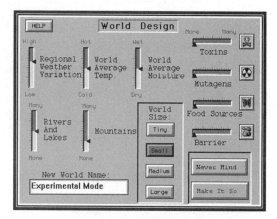

Figure 8.8.

*The World Design
window enables
you to fine-tune
your world.*

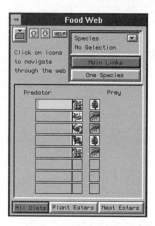

Figure 8.9.

*By checking the
Food Web infor-
mation window,
you can see
which life forms
are consuming
others.*

NOTE: If you can afford only one educational program for your
computer, SimLife should be the one. You can spend many
hours experimenting with worlds and life forms that exist
only within the silicon chips of your computer. There is a
good reason why SimLife has won as many awards as it has:
It's one of the finest educational programs ever written for a
personal computer.

Home Medical Advisor

In Chapter 5, "The Silicon Brain: Artificial Intelligence," you learned about various types of artificial intelligence, one of which was expert systems, which can provide information and advice on just about any area of knowledge. Although expert systems are not a-life in the same sense that a computer virus or a robot is, they do fill in for a human expert. And last I heard, human experts were considered living beings!

One of the most useful applications for expert systems is providing medical help. Using a medical expert system, one can receive medical advice and even diagnose illness. And although no computer program is a substitute for a real doctor, a medical expert system enables you to learn more about various aspects of the medical profession, as well as obtain information about treatments you are receiving, drugs you have been prescribed, injuries you have suffered, and much more.

If nothing else, browsing through a medical expert system is a fascinating way to kill an hour or two. Pixel Perfect, Inc. has released a home medical expert system, called Home Medical Advisor, that provides all the previously listed services, and more.

Home Medical Advisor comes in both a DOS and Windows version—both programs provide extensive knowledge bases covering symptoms, diseases, injuries, medical testing, drugs, poisons, and diet. Each knowledge base is fully indexed so you can find information quickly and easily. In fact, the symptoms section, which is the heart of the program (Figure 8.10), provides not only a complete index, but also human figures on which you can click with your mouse to jump to symptoms related to specific parts of the body.

For example, if you need information on back pain, you first click the figure's back, and then select the specific topic from the generated list. When you select a topic, Home Medical Advisor quickly finds and loads the appropriate information file, displaying it on-screen in a window (Figure 8.11), with possible causes for your symptoms listed at the bottom. By clicking a cause, you can skip the diagnostic question-and-answer session and instead receive immediate information on any of the listed possibilities. In addition, buttons on the windows enable you to maneuver easily forward and backward through previously accessed windows, receive help on using Home Medical Advisor, jump back to the main screen, quit

the program, or initiate the question-and-answer session through which Home Medical Advisor attempts to diagnose your problem.

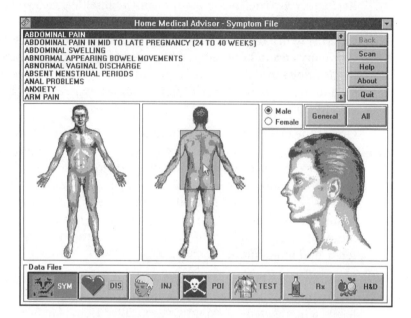

Figure 8.10.

Home Medical Advisor's symptoms section can diagnose illness.

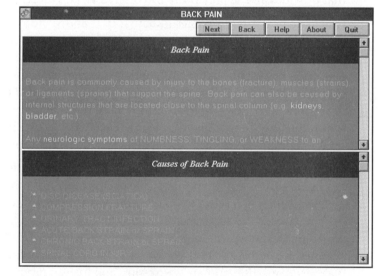

Figure 8.11.

When you select a symptom, Home Medical Advisor displays an information window.

Clicking the Next button initiates the diagnostic section of the program. At this point, Home Medical Advisor asks a series of yes or no questions, using your answers to diagnose your problem.

A colorful VGA image accompanies each question (Figure 8.12), and the questions are easily answered by clicking a Yes or No button. Moreover, if you decide to change an answer, you can use the Back button to trace back through the questioning to any point.

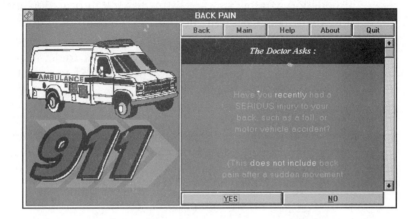

Figure 8.12.

Home Medical Advisor asks a series of questions in order to diagnose an illness.

After you've answered the necessary questions, Home Medical Advisor displays a possible diagnosis (Figure 8.13). As you read the text, you see words displayed in green. You can click these words to jump instantly to another window containing information about the selected word. In any case, all windows contain the Back button, which enables you to trace back to any point in the diagnosis.

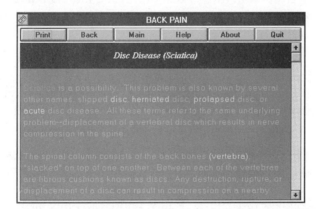

Figure 8.13.

After you answer the "doctor's" questions, Home Medical Advisor displays a possible diagnosis.

Although the symptoms section is the heart of Home Medical Advisor, the disease, injury, test, drug, poison, and diet knowledge bases, too, place a wealth of medical information at your fingertips (or mouse tip, as the case may be).

You can jump to any of the knowledge bases by clicking the appropriate button at the bottom of the main screen. When you do, an introduction window appears, listing general information about the chosen knowledge base. In addition, an index for the knowledge base appears at the top of the screen. You can scroll through the index or use the program's Scan button to locate topics related to a specific word in the knowledge base. In any case, after you locate the topic of interest, clicking it brings up the associated information file.

Home Medical Advisor is a valuable addition to any software library. Thanks to its careful organization and hypercard-like structure, you can find information on most medical topics in a flash. In the case of an emergency, it might even save someone's life.

Virtual Reality Studio 2.0

In Chapter 7, "Worlds of Imagination: Virtual Reality," you had a chance to fly around inside a small virtual world. The program that gave you your wings was created with Domark's Virtual Reality Studio 2.0 (VRS2), a desktop virtual reality editor that enables you to create your own virtual worlds and move around in them any way you want. You can even create 3-D video games with Virtual Reality Studio.

VRS2's editor (Figure 8.14) is where you put together the objects that make up your world, using predefined shapes such as cubes, pyramids, quads, triangles, lines, flexicubes, and more. Using these shapes, you can assemble just about any type of virtual object you can imagine, from a simple floating cube to a complex mansion.

You control VRS2 with your mouse, selecting commands from the menu bar at the top of the screen or clicking buttons in the control panel at the bottom of the screen. Although VRS2 is a fairly complex program, a detailed tutorial accompanies the manual. In addition, a videotape tutorial, which provides a quick tour through VRS2's main features, comes free with the program.

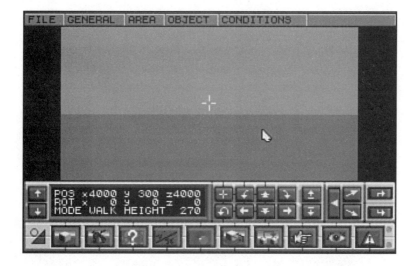

Figure 8.14.

You can use Virtual Reality Studio's editor to create your own virtual worlds.

Still, creating a virtual world with VRS2 (or any VR world editor) is a time-consuming and meticulous task. Each shape in your world must be placed at specific coordinates so they combine to form the objects you want. For example, to build a simple house, you must first position a cube somewhere in the VR world. Next, you must place a pyramid shape, which is the roof, just above the cube. This means setting the pyramid's coordinates so the pyramid seems to rest on top of the cube. You must position the windows and doors in a similar fashion, with each shape being placed at its appropriate coordinates.

Besides its coordinates, you can make each shape in your VR world any color or size you need. Objects also have a variety of characteristics that can make your VR world more dynamic (Figure 8.15). You can make objects invisible, make them movable by the user, make them intangible (meaning the object seems solid but isn't), draw them as wire-frame shapes, and much more. You can even set objects to transport a user to a new location when the user collides with the object. You might, for example, want to make the door to a house a transporter, so when the user hits it, he is transported to a new area representing the inside of the house.

As mentioned previously, you can use VRS2 to create 3-D video games. To this end, you can animate objects in your VR world and have them destroyed when shot by the player. Putting together a video game is more complicated than just positioning objects, of course. You also have to write short pieces of program code with VRS2's built-in programming language. Luckily, you don't have to be a professional programmer to see results. The language (called Freescape Command Language) is easy to learn and apply. VRS2's manual even includes a mini-programming tutorial to help you.

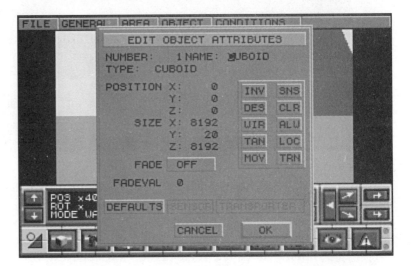

Figure 8.15.

Objects in a VRS2 virtual world can have a variety of characteristics.

When you have finished creating your world, you can use VRS2's Make utility to create a *stand-alone program* (a program that runs without VRS2) that you can distribute to your friends. VRS2 supplies the view window for the stand-alone program, but you must use a paint program to draw the rest of the screen graphics. (In the sample program on your disk, these graphics look like the controls of a spacecraft. VRS2 also supplies other border graphics you can use.)

You can place the controls for manipulating the VR world anywhere you like on-screen, and then use VRS2's control editor (Figure 8.16) to match the controls to the specific screen coordinates. Most controls you need are already set up in the editor; all you must do is tell the editor where the controls should be positioned on-screen, so that they respond to mouse clicks.

Virtual Reality Studio 2.0 is a program you can get lost in for hours at a time. Although building a VR world is a meticulous process, the results are worth the effort. At the least, you'll appreciate the effort that goes into creating 3-D video games.

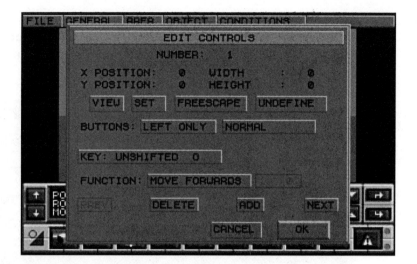

Figure 8.16.

Using the control editor, you can place the controls for your VR world anywhere on-screen.

Ultima Underworld

If you like computer games and also are curious about desktop virtual reality, you should trot down to your nearest software store and check out Origin's ground-breaking Ultima Underworld series of *role-playing games* (RPGs). Particularly terrific is Ultima Underworld II: Labyrinth of Worlds. In this adventure, Lord British's castle has been completely enclosed in a huge blackrock gem, and it's up to you, as the mighty Avatar, to explore beneath the castle to find a way to release the castle's occupants from their terrifying captivity.

Ultima Underworld's claim to fame is its 3-D first-person viewpoint (Figure 8.17), which is the best in the industry. In Ultima Underworld's VR world, as with Virtual Reality Studio, you can look in any direction, including up and down, and see a realistic representation of the current scene from your new angle. However, the graphics are much more detailed than those found in Virtual Reality Studio—these graphics even feature animated creatures that you must fight in *real-time battle*. (Real-time battle is continuous-action battle, rather than turn-based battle.)

Lord British's castle, as well as the dungeons and other worlds to which you travel, are well populated with all manner of life, from human allies that can teach you important skills to horrible monsters who would like nothing better than to reduce you to scrap meat and bone. You can converse with most of the intelligent creatures (Figure 8.18), gaining new information and even trading for helpful items. Choose your topics of conversation carefully, though, or you might find yourself in more trouble than a mouse on a freeway!

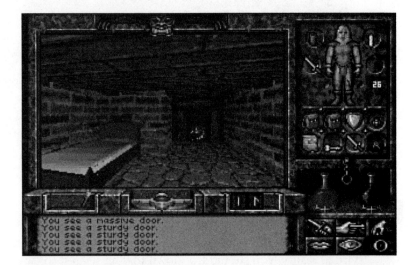

Figure 8.17.

Origin's 3-D, first-person viewpoint dungeon games are the best in the industry.

Figure 8.18.

You can converse with many of the other characters in the game.

As with all RPGs, your character has attributes that change as you play (Figure 8.19). For example, the STR attribute is your strength, DEX is your dexterity, INT is your intelligence, EXP is your experience, and VIT is your health (vitality). Each of these basic attributes affects your character's abilities and the way he acts in specific situations.

Figure 8.19.

In Ultima Underworld, your character has attributes that affect his abilities.

Besides his attributes, your character has a number of skills that you can improve throughout the game, including spell casting, combat, lock picking, swimming, bartering, and repairing broken items. To improve a skill, you must earn *experience* (which advances your character's level) and *skill points* (which you use to purchase training from an instructor). An important element of the game is knowing which skills are most important to your playing strategy.

As you explore the dungeons beneath Lord British's castle and gather the correct items, you gain access to eight new worlds, including such exotic locales as the Ice Caverns, the Pits of Carnage, the Ethereal Void, the Prison Tower, and Loth's Tomb. Each of these areas comprises many rooms, corridors, and tunnels that you must explore. To help you keep track of your current location, Ultima Underworld II boasts an auto-mapping feature (Figure 8.20) that automatically generates a map as you explore. You can even add your own notes to the map.

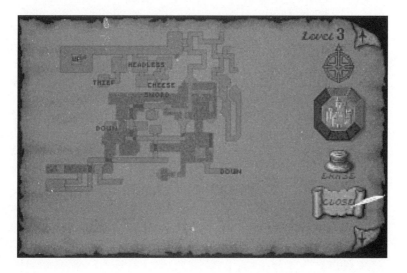

Figure 8.20.

Ultima Underworld's automatic mapping makes it easy to keep track of your location.

Most important for an RPG, though, is the story. Origin's games have always had strong story lines, and Ultima Underworld II is no exception. From the moment you first set foot in Lord British's castle until you manage to solve the game's many puzzles and free the castle, you follow the story's plot from one point to the next as you discover secrets, question people (and creatures), and travel from world to world. In the game's main story line, sundry subplots enrich the unfolding tale, bringing other characters in the game to life.

After you begin playing Ultima Underworld II, though, you might have a hard time pulling yourself away. There is always one more corridor to explore, one more dungeon to map, one more puzzle to solve. You can expect to spend over 100 hours hunched over your keyboard before you reach the end of the game. And when you reach the end, you'll feel as you do when you finish a good book— wanting more and anxious for the sequel. (Luckily, in the computer-game world, most successful games have sequels.)

There are several other dungeon exploring games on the market, but the Ultima Underworld series is the cream of the crop. You'll be amazed at how realistic a computer-generated fantasy world can be.

Conclusion

The programs reviewed here are only a few suggestions—some of the better products this author discovered over the course of researching this book. Your local software dealer stocks many other packages that incorporate elements of a-life. Maxis, for example, has also released SimEarth, a simulation that focuses on the effects of environment on life; and El-Fish, which enables you to breed computer-generated tropical fish with which to stock an on-screen fish tank. In addition, many computer games use desktop VR techniques to create their displays, most notably Microsoft's classic Flight Simulator. You can find also several types of expert systems at your local software store.

Whichever programs you choose, your computing experience will be richer thanks to the efforts of the dedicated researchers working in the fields of artificial life, artificial intelligence, and virtual reality. Think of them the next time you sit down behind your computer.

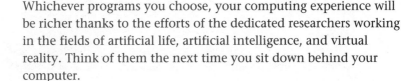

A Brave and Uncertain New World: The Future of Artificial Life

When Christopher Langton arranged the first artificial life conference in 1987, he suspected that there were many people throughout the world studying and experimenting with artificial life. Because the study of artificial life was not yet a formal discipline, however, these researchers were mostly unaware of each other. Unable to share their discoveries, researchers likely were performing duplicate work, which in turn slowed the field's advancement.

Langton hoped the time had come to bring these researchers together—to formalize their field of study. He had no idea how many people might respond to the conference's announcement. In his worst-case scenario, he would have a conference hall filled with crackpots. Still, he took the chance, and, luckily, Langton's instincts

were correct. The conference was a rousing success. It attracted about 160 researchers, most of whom brought fascinating examples of artificial life.

But once the proceedings got under way, it was apparent that not only did researchers in the field of a-life need to pool their knowledge and resources, but they needed also to set up guidelines within which they could perform further research safely and ethically. After all, when dealing with any form of life, whether it be natural or human-made, one must follow a code of ethics. In the conference's published proceedings, Langton writes:

> [Moral and ethical] issues must be discussed before we go much further down the road to creating life artificially. We are once again at a point where our technical grasp of a problem is far ahead of our moral understanding of the issues involved, or of the possible consequences of mastering the technology.

Are artificial life forms actually alive? If they are, do these artificial life forms have the same right to life as any other living being? Because humans create a life form doesn't necessarily mean that humans have a right to destroy it. And how about self-replication? The reproductive capabilities of some a-life makes it imperative that humankind retain control over a-life after it's created. Imagine, for example, a particularly nasty computer virus. In this age of digital information, such a virus can bring the world to its knees.

At this early stage in the study of artificial life, many of these concerns might seem unimportant. Certainly, no computer has yet displayed a form of a-life that one can classify as living. And, although computer viruses are destructive, even causing millions of dollars worth of damage, they are a long way from being uncontrollable. Still, according to Langton, a-life is destined to become an important part of a new biosphere that includes traditional and artificial life forms. Humans will have to develop a new culture that encourages the development of a symbiotic relationship between biological life and a-life.

Other researchers agree with Langton. Doyne Farmer says, within the next century, living organisms created by humans will almost certainly be a part of our world. These human-made organisms will

have the capability to reproduce and evolve. Hans Moravec believes that fully intelligent robots will be common within 50 years. Moravec further theorizes that humans will someday be forced to transfer their minds into supercomputers and leave their bodies— the weakest link in the chain of human existence—behind once and for all. Rodney Brooks envisions a future world in which tiny, insect-like robots will not only manicure your lawn, but also travel through your bloodstream, repairing arteries and performing other medical services.

These researchers all have different views of the future, but they agree that a-life is not only possible, but also inevitable. Will the day come when humans must share their world with strange new residents? According to the finest scientific minds in the field, the answer is an unequivocal yes.

The Dark Side

"It is natural to fear the unknown, particularly when it involves a threat to our species," wrote Doyne Farmer and a colleague, Alletta Belin, in *Artificial Life II,* the proceedings of the Second Artificial Life Workshop. "It is easy to imagine nightmare scenarios in which cold, malevolent machines or vicious genetically engineered creatures overwhelm humanity."

If this quotation doesn't run a shiver down your spine, you better read it again. The destructive potential of a-life is something with which humans must reckon, especially if the past has any lessons to teach. The fact is, the scientific community does not always act within the boundaries of reasonable safety. For example, when scientists detonated the first atomic bomb, they were not absolutely sure they could stop the chain reaction. According to some scientists, there was a remote chance that the bomb would ignite the entire atmosphere, burning uncontrollably. So, you might ask, why did they conduct these experiments? Because the world was at war and the United States was desperate to develop the ultimate weapon with which to end the war. Necessity, although it is often the mother of invention, also can be the mother of extinction.

In fact, the parallel between the development of the atomic bomb and the development of a-life is more apt than you might at first believe. Military applications for a-life include everything from robot soldiers to intelligent satellites capable of waging war from the vacuum of space. It's no coincidence that a-life researchers, especially in the field of robotics and computer viruses, frequently receive funding from the government. Doyne Farmer, for one, fears that self-reproducing war machines will be capable not only of winning a war, but also of destroying their creators in the process.

It is an eerie coincidence that the Los Alamos National Laboratory, the birthplace of artificial life as a science, is also the place where scientists developed the atomic bomb. Although the first detonation of an atomic bomb did not, after all, burn beyond control and destroy the planet, the threat of nuclear destruction remains with us today. Might a-life be yet another threat to human survival?

An Excerpt From...

Steven Levy...

In his excellent book *Artificial Life: The Quest for a New Creation*, Steven Levy writes:

> *By utilizing the biological mechanics that allow natural life to evolve according to its own rules of fitness, one invariably creates organisms that operate according to their own needs, whether or not these happen to correspond to their creator's needs. This quality allows artificial organisms to discover perpetually innovative solutions to the problems researchers pose to them, but it also flirts with the risk that the organisms will mutate in a manner that will make them, in effect, ask themselves why they should bother to do what the researchers want them to do.*

Scary stuff. The day might come when human-made creatures decide they have no further need for humans. The results of this decision will depend on the nature of the life form. Maybe they'll treat us, their creators, with the reverence granted only to gods; maybe they'll suffer our existence for their own amusement; or maybe they'll decide the world is better off without us. It's easy to shrug off such scenarios as science-fiction horror stories, but to do so is to ignore real danger that lurks just beyond a distant horizon.

Into the Light

But, although a-life harbors deadly potential, it also provides an equally powerful hope for the future. Artificial life forms can take on many important new roles in a future world.

"Good" computer viruses, for example, can be used to fight and destroy "bad" computer viruses, in much the same way vaccinations have eradicated the disease smallpox from the planet. One would inject these immunological viruses into a computer network, and, silently and unobtrusively, the viruses would spread from computer to computer, wiping out destructive viruses as they go. The anti-viruses would soon become a part of every operating system they "infected," providing permanent protection.

Programmers at the Lawrence Livermore Laboratory have already created such antiviruses. However, because they are unsure of the full effects of releasing such a virus, the programmers have kept their creation under wraps.

Another scientist, Harold Thimbleby, a computer scientist at Scotland's Stirling University, is working on what he calls *liveware,* virus-like computer organisms that can perform certain tasks automatically. Thimbleby has already used his liveware to create an auto-updating database. This database virus works by examining copies of the same database and determining whether both copies are equally up to date, making the required additions if not.

Fred Cohen, credited with creating the first computer virus (an experimental virus that he did not allow to escape its local computer environment), also has created a beneficent computer virus. Cohen's virus monitors a bill-collection system, generating reminders and demands at appropriate times with no help from a human operator. Cohen also has created a virus that monitors its host system, checking file access clearance and cleaning up "dead" viruses (Cohen's viruses have limited life spans).

Another new application for computer a-life is *self-improving programs.* Using genetic algorithms to pass on successful traits to new generations, computer programs can compete against each other for survival, the goal being to find the best solution to a programming problem. Programs that solve the problem best are deemed most fit and so survive to reproduce, passing their clever algorithms on to their "children."

In the less immediate future, even more spectacular forms of a-life will appear. It's impossible to predict what these artificial creatures will be like, but one can speculate. For example, a-life forms might someday explore the galaxy, looking for new homes for the human race. In science fiction stories, planets are often made habitable through a process known as *terra forming*. Using terra forming, a-life creatures could clean and modify an inhospitable planet's atmosphere so to support life. In addition, these creatures could re-engineer the planet to represent the surface of the Earth.

Currently, such a huge task is beyond comprehension, but what if humans could develop artificial life forms that travel between planets, shuttling terra-forming materials from one planet to another and installing those materials at the new site? Although it would require millions of such creatures to complete such a complex process, humans would need to create only a few. The rest could be produced through self-replication.

This idea of using a self-replicating machine to resculpt the universe is nothing new. In the book *2010: Odyssey II,* a sequel to the famous *2001: A Space Odyssey,* an alien creation (the monolith) replicates until it consumes the entire planet of Jupiter, eventually transforming the planet into a new sun. This new sun thaws the frozen moon Europa, and thus begins the evolution of a new life form that had been trapped beneath the moon's ice for eons.

The Brave New World

Whichever types of a-life our scientists create, there's little question that the future will be a different place indeed. If researchers in the field of artificial intelligence have their way, within the next century our descendants will see computers, robots, and other a-life imbued with truly human minds. On the other hand, if the quest for human-like artificial intelligence turns into a dead end, a-life forms might be more like those Rodney Brooks envisioned, insect-like robots that perform their tasks mindlessly—and relentlessly.

In any case, an artificial life form need not be intelligent to be useful to the human race. Neither need it be intelligent to replace humans as the dominant life form on this planet. Truth is, there are those who argue that intelligence is not a survival trait, but rather the beginning of a long evolutionary spiral into oblivion. Human intelligence may, after all, lead us to create our own successors.

Bibliography

The following is a list of all published sources used in the writing of this book. It serves not only as an acknowledgment to all the folks whose work made this author's job easier, but also as a reading list for readers who wish to learn more about artificial life and related topics. The three "must read" volumes listed are *Artificial Life* and *Artificial Life II*, the proceedings of the first and second a-life conferences, both edited by Christopher Langton, and *Artificial Life, The Quest for a New Creation*, by Stephen Levy.

Nonfiction

Amato, Ivan. "Inventing Life." *Science News*, May 19, 1990, pp. 312-314.

Beer, Randall D., Hillel J. Chiel, and Leon S. Sterling. "An Artificial Insect." *American Scientist*, September-October 1991. pp. 444-452.

Bundy, Alan. "What Kind of Field is AI?" *Foundations of AI: A Source Book*, ed. Derek Partridge and Yorick Wilks. Cambridge, U.K.: Cambridge University Press, 1990.

Daviss, Bennett. "Technology 1990: Laid-Back Computers." *Discover*, January 1991, pp. 60-61.

Dery, Mark. "Terminators." *Rolling Stone*, June 10th, 1993, pp. 14-21+.

Dewdney, A.K. "Turing Test." *Scientific American,* January 1992, pp. 30-32.

Dewdney, A.K. "Insectoids Invade a Field of Robots." *Scientific American,* July 1991, pp. 118-121.

Dewdney, A.K. "Photovores." *Scientific American,* September 1992, pg. 42.

Dworetzky, Tom. "MechAnimals." *Omni,* March 1991, pp. 50-54+.

Edelhart, Mike. "The Cradle of Artificial Life." *PC Computing,* February 1991, pp. 152-155.

Elmer-Dewitt, Philip. "In Search of Artificial Life." *Time,* August 6, 1990, pg. 64.

Elmer-Dewitt, Philip. "Ding! Whrrrrrrrrrrrr. Crash!" *Time,* March 16, 1992, pg. 56.

Engelberger, Joseph F. *Robotics in Service.* Cambridge, MA: The MIT Press, 1989.

Farmer, J. Doyne and Alletta d'A. Belin. "Artificial Life: The Coming Evolution." *Artificial Life II,* ed. Christopher G. Langton, Charles Taylor, J. Doyne Farmer, and Steen Rasmussen. New York: Addison Wesley, 1992.

Fites, Philip, Peter Johnston, and Martin Kratz. *The Computer Virus Crisis.* New York: Van Nostrand Reinhold, 1989.

Flam, Faye. "Swarms of Mini-Robots Set To Take on Mars Terrain." *Science.* September 18, 1992, pg. 1621.

Forsyth, Richard, and Chris Naylor. *The Hitch-hiker's Guide to Artificial Intelligence.* New York: Chapman and Hall/Methuen, 1985.

Freedman, David H. "Invasion of the Insect Robots." *Discover,* March 1991, pp. 42-50.

Hayward, Tom. *Adventures in Virtual Reality.* Carmel, IN: Que Corporation, 1993.

Hinton, Geoffrey E. "How Neural Networks Learn from Experience." *Scientific American,* September 1992, pp. 145-151.

Hunt, V. Daniel. *Understanding Robotics.* New York: Academic Press, 1990.

Johnson, J.T. "Fuzzy Logic." *Popular Science*, July 1990, pp. 87-89.

Langton, Christopher G. ed. *Artificial Life.* New York: Addison-Wesley, 1989.

Langton, Christopher G., Charles Taylor, J. Doyne Farmer, and Steen Rasmussen, eds. *Artificial Life II.* New York: Addison-Wesley, 1992.

Lee, Mark H. *Intelligent Robotics.* New York: Halsted Press, 1989.

Levy, Steven. "It's Alive!" *Rolling Stone,* June 13, 1991, pp. 89-92.

Levy, Steven. *Artificial Life, The Quest for a New Creation.* New York: Pantheon Books, 1992.

McAfee, John, and Colin Haynes. *Computer Viruses, Worms, Data Diddlers, Killer Programs, and Other Threats to Your System.* New York: St. Martin's Press, 1989.

Miller, Michael J. "It's Alive!" *PC Magazine,* May 25, 1993, pp. 81-82.

Minsky, Marvin, ed. *Robotics.* Garden City, NY: Anchor Press/Doubleday, 1985.

O'Malley, Christopher. "Stalking Stealth Viruses." *Popular Science,* January 1993, pp. 54-58+.

Ramus, Daniel W. "Putting the Experts to Work." *Byte,* January 1991, pp. 281-287.

Regis, Ed and Tom Dworetzky. "Child of a Lesser God." *Omni,* October 1988, pp. 92-96+.

Regis, Ed. "Interview: Christopher Langton." *Omni,* October 1991, pp. 99-134.

Rogers, Michael, with Bob Conn. "Not Too Much of a Headache." *Newsweek,* March 16, 1992, pg. 64.

Ryan, Bob. "AI's Identity Crisis." *Byte,* January 1991, pp. 239-246.

Schank, Roger C. "What is AI Anyway?" *The AI Magazine*, Vol. 8, No. 4, 1987.

Scheck, Susan. "Is It Live or Is It Memory?" *Technology Review,* April 1991, pp.13-14.

Simons, Geoff. *Are Computers Alive?* Boston: Birkhäuser, 1983.

Stein, Richard Marlon. "Real Artificial Life." *Byte,* January 1991, pp. 289-298.

Taylor, Wendy. "Virus-Proof Your PC." *PC/Computing,* February 1992, pp. 122-124.

Thompson, Bill, and Bev Thompson. "Overturning the Category Bucket." *Byte,* January 1991, pp. 249-256.

Travis, John. "Electronic Ecosystem." *Science News,* August 10, 1991, pp. 88-90.

Turing, Alan M. "Computing Machinery and Intelligence." *Mind,* 59 (1950), pp. 433-460.

Wallich, P. "Silicon Babies." *Scientific American,* December 1991, pp. 125-134.

Winston, Patrick Henry. *Artificial Intelligence.* New York: Addison Wesley, 1992.

Yeaple, Judith Anne. "Go Robots, Go!" *Popular Science,* December 1992, pp.96-102+.

Fiction

Asimov, Isaac. *The Complete Robot.* Garden City, New York: Doubleday, 1982.

Bear, Greg. *Blood Music.* New York: Arbor House, 1985.

Clarke, Arthur C. *2001: A Space Odyssey.* New York: ROC, 1968.

Clarke, Arthur C. *2010: Odyssey II.* New York: Del Rey Books, 1982.

Hogan, James P. *Code of the Life Maker.* New York: Ballantine Books, 1983.

Index

INDEX

A

acoustic sensors (robots), 110-111
activating
    Game of Life (DOS version), 28
    PLife, 31
activation phase (computer virus), 74
AI (artificial intelligence), 83-84, 87-88
    Applied AI, 84
    basic AI, 84
    brain comparison, 88-89
    characteristics, 87
    cognitive science, 84
    expert systems, 89-93, 97-100
        Fish Expert System, 98-100
        Guess the Animal game, 93-97
        neural networks, 91
        rule-based, 92
    fuzzy logic, 90
    hybrid systems, 90-91
    neural networks, 89, 91
alarm scents (SimAnt), 152
algorithms, 6
    testing effectiveness, 12
    see also, genetic algorithms

Ant Hall of Fame (MicroAnts), 62
Anti-Virus (Central Point), 77
AntiVirus (Norton), 77
antiviruses, 171
Applied AI, 84
ArtAnt, 25
artifical life workshop (Langton), 21
artifical selection, 27
artificial intelligence, see AI
Artificial Life: The Quest for a New Creation, 170
asexual reproduction, 48
Asimov, Isaac, 2
    Three Laws of Robitics, 103
Attila (robot bug), 116
auto industry robots, 106
automata
    cellular, 39
    finite-state, 6, 37-39

T

U-V

W

X–Y–Z

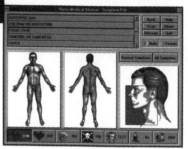

Installing the Disk!

Before you can use the programs included on this book's disk, you must install them onto your hard drive. To do this, follow these instructions:

1. At the DOS prompt, type C: to switch to your hard drive, then type **CD ** to move to the drive's root directory.

2. Insert the book disk into drive A.

3. Type **COPY A:\ALIFE.EXE** to copy the file containing the book's programs to your drive C.

4. Type **ALIFE** to decompress the book's program files.

After following this procedure, you will have a directory called ALIFE on your drive C. This directory contains all the programs featured in this book, each in its own subdirectory. Instructions for running the programs are in the chapters in which the programs are discussed. In addition, a description of each program is included in the book's introduction.
